DISCARDED

Bargaining at the
Local Level

BARGAINING AT THE LOCAL LEVEL

John J. Collins

NEW YORK
FORDHAM UNIVERSITY PRESS
1974

© Copyright 1974 by FORDHAM UNIVERSITY PRESS
All rights reserved.
ISBN 0–8232–0972–5
LC 73–81503

Printed in the United States of America

TO
"PAT" JOHNSTON
WHO LOVED LIFE FOR ITS GOODNESS,
WHO PURSUED TRUTH RELENTLESSLY,
WHOSE WHOLESOMENESS WAS AS ADMIRED
AS HER LAUGHTER WAS INFECTIOUS.
THOSE OF US WHO SHARE THESE MEMORIES
ARE THE FORTUNATE ONES.

ACKNOWLEDGMENTS

Despite the author's familiarity with this subject, based on extensive participation in local-level bargaining, it would be the height of folly, to say nothing of lack of humility, if one were to write a book such as this and not recognize how dependent one is on others.

There is no way to thank specifically all those who both provided ideas and read bits and pieces of this effort as it was being put together. So I will make a "general confession" of indebtedness and express my sincere gratitude for both their interest and their ideas.

But in every work that requires research there are particular people whose help has been invaluable. These I would like to thank individually because it is from their knowledge as well as their courtesy that much of the material which appears here has been made possible. To Anne M. Murphy, Director of Libraries at Fordham University, whose ever gracious assistance makes one feel that she is the recipient of that assistance rather than the reverse; to Mary Winterle, Industrial Relations Counsellors, whose intimate knowledge of the various source materials for labor relations enabled the author to pursue pertinent data relating to independent-union studies.

In the academic world, I am especially grateful to William Grace, Professor of English, and to John C. Olin, Professor of History, at Fordham University, for examining several chapters and for their helpful suggestions; to T. K. Meier, who gave the author the benefit of his editorial skill; to my colleague, F. W. Schmidt, Lecturer in History, Fordham University, and a knowledgeable editor in the field of textbooks, whose suggestions as well as specific corrections have contributed to whatever style this effort may possess; to Walter Hartmeyer whose inherent skepticism helped the author to avoid making assumptions at critical points.

I wish particularly to extend my thanks to Floyd Curtis who has lived with this subject for many years. His contribution in addition to occasional typing was his insistence on accuracy. His careful research of independent union documents proved most profitable. To Carlota Jouvin for her encouragement and to Diane Toelk for having the information needed readily available and for doing the many chores that were part and parcel of its preparation.

But above all, were it not for the hundreds of hours of typing and retyping done so graciously and so well by a wonderful person, Betty LaMothe, this would not have seen the light of day. Not only did she with good humor accept numerous revisions, but she acted as a sounding board regarding structure and style. Her willingness to listen to the author's musings on what the manuscript should contain and what conveniently could be eliminated provided a very special kind of guidance. Thank you, Betty.

Contents

	Introduction	1
1	Has Local-Level Bargaining Worked?	17
2	Bargaining on Pensions—The Mobil Approach	40
3	More on Pension Bargaining—Texaco Does It Differently	58
4	The Humble Way	64
5	Difficulties But No Doubts	76
6	The Role of the Executive Committee	87
7	Comparing the Economic Package	100
8	Settling Grievances	111
9	Seniority—Its Necessity and Its Fragility	124
10	A Wide Range of Interests	133
11	Differences Between 'Independents' and 'Nationals'	150
12	Problems of Big Labor	167
	Conclusion	183
	Index	189

SELECTED ABBREVIATIONS

ATOA	American Tanker Officers Association
DOA	Deepwater Officers Association
GTOA	Getty Tanker Officers Association
JSTOA	Jersey Standard Tanker Officers Association
MEBA	Marine Engineers Beneficial Association
MTOA	Mobil Tanker Officers Association
TROA	Texaco Radio Officers Association
TTOA	Texaco Tanker Officers Association

Bargaining at the Local Level

Introduction

"LET US ONLY SUFFER ANY PERSON to tell us his story, morning and evening, but for one twelve month, and he will become our master." These words of Edmund Burke from his essay "The War with Jacobin France" could be used to suit any situation where simple repetition is employed to sell a product, an idea or even a political candidate. The story of the national affiliated unions has been told over and over again. And while occasionally critical, generally speaking, the accounts in textbooks, magazines, and newspapers have been on the positive side. The assumption has been that these are the *only* unions in existence. This is understandable because of the importance of Big Labor in the current economic climate—especially since they have organized successfully such major industries as automobile, steel, rubber and transportation; and when they call a strike, the economy, or large segments of it, comes to a grinding halt. Even politically they appear to be a power through their lobbying strength in Congress, in state legislatures, and in city councils.

There is nothing inherently wrong in this. In fact, there have been some employers in the past and there will be some in the future for whom the force of powerful unions is the only language they understand. Certainly employees should not be denied the opportunity of seeking this type of representation. And the George Meanys and the Peter Brennans should be heard in and out of legislative chambers, since they do speak for many whose voices need the amplification that the large labor unions can supply.

But when the student of labor problems, and the various Federal and State agencies and the news media are deprived of sources of information on successful bargaining except that which comes via Big Labor, someone should set the record straight. Otherwise Burke's words may become a reality and the so-called Labor Movement could become the monolithic political power that Walter Reuther and those who believe as he did wish it to become.

Local-level bargaining accomplished via the independent union is the antithesis of industry-wide bargaining. Local-level bargaining, because it is just that, is not about to be written up in magazines; nor is a description of it to be found in high school or college textbooks. The only time it will be mentioned in the newspaper is that rare situation where an independent union in a key industry or a large company is on strike. If something does not cause waves, it is not news. This is particularly true of labor events. No newspaper would have sufficient pages to print all the arguments offered, the impasses reached and recesses taken, that are so much a part of the everyday bargaining process.

But there is the need for the student of labor in the United States and for public and quasi-public bodies, including the news media, to be aware that, as in other aspects of American society, i.e., education and religion—labor unionism is pluralistic; that there is no specific form of labor organization that has all the answers to the economic and other problems of employees in this country, any more than there is a particular form of education suited to all students in the country.

There must be freedom to choose whatever instrument any particular group believes will best achieve their objectives. A corollary of this freedom to choose is the obligation—whenever and wherever the situation requires—of the news media, educators, and government officials to make as many people as possible aware of the pluralistic nature of our society. And this includes the pluralism of labor organization.

Here, it must be admitted, local-level bargaining as represented by independent unions is in a dilemma. In a general way it wants the public to know of its existence but in another sense it treasures its privacy. What it does not want is the imputation that because its membership is limited to the employees of a particular company it is somehow company-dominated. This "damning with faint praise" it can do without. It is even worse than "benign neglect."

In 1933 and 1934, William Green, then president of the AFL and John L. Lewis, president of the United Mine Workers, had some very unkind words to say about the then-current form of local-level bargaining, Employee Representation Plans.[1] They called them company unions. Because there were no dues and the employer had initiated them to deal collectively with his employees they were considered by some to be completely outside the mainstream of the American labor movement. And they were—if one considered the AFL the mainstream of organized labor, which it was. But the real reason for the dislike of Employee Representation Plans by organized (AFL-organized) labor at that time, was

INTRODUCTION 3

the *competition* they were getting from this form of employee organization. According to studies made in 1932 and 1933 by the National Industrial Conference Board, more than two million employees were dealing with their employers through this medium—compared with a total of approximately three million members in AFL unions.[2] Furthermore the bulk of AFL membership was in the construction and clothing industries. There were few AFL unions in the auto industry, in steel and non-ferrous metals. There were none in the petroleum industry. In fact, in practically all manufacturing it would be difficult to find AFL unions in 1932.

As the economy and the law changed and new social objectives developed, the Employee Representation Plan as a vehicle for employees to deal collectively with the employer was modified to become the philosophical father of later local-level bargaining done via independent unions. But in the early days of the New Deal employee representation as it then prevailed was marked for oblivion. This was made abundantly clear by the testimony given before the Senate Labor Committee that in 1934–1935 was holding hearings on a bill which when passed (July 5, 1935) became the famous Wagner Act. It was this act that outlawed company-dominated unions which were considered to be such if the employer provided any kind of financial assistance however slight or oblique.[3]

At the time some of the more articulate leaders of the AFL, plus doctrinaire liberals, were looking to the day when the unorganized would be organized. They did not have long to wait. In 1934, as the New Deal was getting underway, John L. Lewis, as leader of the United Mine Workers, marched ten unions out of the AFL to become the basis of the Committee for Industrial Organizations (CIO). Under the protection of the Wagner Act, this new and militant labor organization began what became the most successful organizing campaign in the history of labor. Its record for a four-year period (1935–1939) never has been equaled. And it did its organizing on an industrial or vertical basis in major manufacturing industries, in exactly the same structured way employees had been gathered together under the now banished Employee Representation Plans.

Among the liberals who had endorsed this interdiction of Employee Representation Plans was David Saposs who, shortly after the National Labor Relations Board was established, found a berth with it. Here he was able more adroitly and effectively to continue his pet project of demolishing any organization whose membership was limited to the employees of one company. His lopsided views were contained in a memorandum entitled "Current Anti-Labor Activities," prepared by the Division of Economic Research, National Labor Relations Board.[4]

It is somewhat ironic that the very industrial structure which had been the framework for the Employee Representation Plan became the basis for CIO (Committee for *Industrial* Organization) unions when they sought to organize the unorganized in steel, autos, etc. And it was this vertical or industrial structure, versus the horizontal or craft structure typified by AFL unions, that was the real reason for the bitter enmity from 1934 to 1955, between these two labor organizations. It also was the reason for the marked success of CIO unions over AFL unions in Labor Board-conducted elections during this period. The fact that the Labor Board leaned toward industrial unions was indicated by the appropriate units they designated (industrial)—which added fuel to the fire that raged between the CIO and AFL and caused the latter to accuse the Labor Board of bias in behalf of the CIO.[5] It was not until 1955 that these twenty-year enemies agreed to bury their differences. The merged organizations became the current AFL-CIO.

It is equally ironic to note the company financial assistance provided, *by contract,* to major CIO unions today in the light of the firm proscription of such assistance that AFL leaders insisted the Wagner Act contain. There is no comparison between the financial assistance given to the United Auto Workers by the automobile manufacturers, approximately $20-million per year for Ford alone[6] —payment of full annual salary to union committee men—and the financial assistance given pre-Wagner Act Employee Representation Plans: a place to meet, some stationery, and a day off once a month for delegates to convene. The position taken by AFL leaders when testifying in behalf of the Wagner Act was that any financial assistance from the company constituted company domination. Today financial assistance to large AFL-CIO unions is coupled with other forms of what is persuasively labeled "union security." But no one in government or out of government (including students of labor relations) calls attention to this fact. It is considered "a cost of doing business"—business with Big Labor. Inasmuch as the income (apart from the direct company financial assistance) of the United Auto Workers is in excess of $100-million a year, one would think that to keep themselves strictly at arms length from the company, they would pay the expenses, including wages— where lost—of their committeemen, especially since the automobile companies have granted the United Auto Workers the union shop which guarantees them complete financial security via payment by all employees of union dues as a condition of continued employment.

There is nothing morally or legally wrong for an employer who deals with a labor union to make a reasonable arrangement whereby employees who act as representatives of their fellow employees not be penalized financially for so acting. But it does seem a little much for a $100-million-per-year organization to have its hand out for a few more million from the companies for whom they have no use, and at the same time have the effrontery to castigate, or have their spokesmen in and out of ivy-covered institutions repeatedly label, local-level unions as "company unions" in the derogatory sense of that expression. This is not merely poor scholarship; it is poor sportsmanship. This incessant debasing of local-level bargaining unfortunately has had its effect. Instead of being praised for the stability it has brought to employer–employee relations, and the substantial economic benefits realized by employees represented by this form of labor organization, local-level bargaining has become for those with a superficial knowledge of it synonymous with weakness—without even an attempt being made to define weakness.

To read the doleful recitals of the dark days ahead for local-level bargaining contained in some studies, to say nothing of the incomprehension of their function in modern employer–employee relations, is discouraging reading. But by analogy with Mark Twain's remark that "The newspaper account of my death is greatly exaggerated," the story of the early demise of the independent union not only is questionable factually but is incompatible with its essence. That essence consists in the belief by employees that since they are an integral part of the company their interests are best served by utilizing a vehicle that confines its membership to existing employees. The independent union is such a vehicle. In addition it can more easily control its internal structure.

The frequent Phoenix-like rise of the "independent" after its opponents were certain it had been destroyed additionally argues to its intrinsic right to exist in order that employees may avail themselves of an instrument of their own creation. This approach may seem beguiling since so little local-level bargaining now exists nationwide. But this misses the point. The philosophical correctness of the integral relation of the three parts of the company, employer, employees and stockholders has little to do with whether at a particular moment any one of those parts is not playing its proper role. The perfect "mix" in this area, or in any area for that matter, is never more than a hope. And by the way, what would happen to civilization itself where hope is absent?

It is the contention of the author that national affiliated unions have a place in American labor, but their place is not representing employees in a particular company—unless the employer has acted in so negative a manner as to impair the possibility for those parts of the company to work in harmony. The niche of national unions is in the crafts, and as representatives of casual labor such as longshoremen and those seamen who choose to work for a wide variety of shipowners. Here they are necessary not only because of the impermanent nature of this employment, but they are valuable in fulfilling that "need to belong," especially acute in these groups. Over the years by a system of negotiated employer contributions and union monitored funds, national unions representing such casual labor, including seamen, have effectively protected their members in adverse times and in the days of their retirement. This is further proof of the existence and the efficacy of pluralism in labor relations.

Local-level bargaining is predicated on a different premise—the existence of a continuing institution, the company. The company is the sum of its parts. None of these parts exists by itself. Their existence assumes a company *in being*. Stockholders must be stockholders in a particular company; management must be the management of that company and employees are employed by that company. It is this author's contention that in modern labor relations there is little recognition of this natural and integral relationship of employees as a unit to the company—at least in the bargaining process. Instead, for the past forty years there has been an acceptance of national unions as the normal representative of employees in collective bargaining. With such commonplace slogans as the "solidarity of labor" and "workers of the world unite," there has developed in the minds of many an unconscious exclusion of local-level bargaining—bargaining within the framework of the company.

It is the author's purpose to emphasize that the nature of the company requires or certainly suggests that the employees collectively, as one of its constituent parts, bargain on the local level. From actual experience with local-level bargaining in the independent union, the author will seek to establish that its viability and its value to the parties directly involved, as well as its stabilizing effect on the general economy, is a fact which has not been sufficiently recognized.

To recapture a concept which is intrinsically sound, but by adverse propaganda has been distorted to appear a tool of management, requires the re-education of two generations—of the mid-1930s and the mid-1970s. But if in the process a clearer understanding of what constitutes local-level bargaining is realized the effort is worth it.

Separated legally from the company (by virtue of the Taft-Hartley Act), creatures solely of the employees who brought them into being, independent unions, by restricting their membership and activities to the employees of a single company or even a division of a company, function as one of the constituent elements of the company. They are a part of a living and continuing institution. They share the same long-range goals as the stockholders and management of the company—success in the marketplace in providing consumers with the goods and services they need—although this is not consciously emphasized. This is one reason why independent unions are different from national unions—different not just in degree but different *in kind*.

Where independent unions are the choice of the employees— after the drama of a labor board election has passed—most employees represented by them accept local-level bargaining as a way of life, provided their leadership continues to be concerned. Such leadership is more necessary for independent unions than for national unions since the latter have a tightly structural organization. Even occasional deviations in the conduct of leaders of national unions or disputes among their hierarchy do not as a rule result in the destruction of their organization.

The leadership of the independent union must possess two qualities to keep the organization on an even keel. One, they must believe firmly and unswervingly in its value and, regardless of its difficulties, never doubt its ability to provide solutions. Two, the leadership must render satisfactory service to the members by recognizing their dignity as individuals, and without demagoguery, employ their judgment to advance the objectives of that membership.

This brief and perhaps ideological description of the independent union may occasion some surprise among students of labor relations because they have been accustomed to treat the independent union as the weak, or even at times the illegitimate, sister of the large national unions. There is a basic difference between a national union and a union comprised only of employees of a particular company. The former usually has hands outstretched to gather in any who seem ripe for organization, with promises of militant action and, of course, instant success. The national union presumes an adversary relationship with the employer and stresses the distance between them.

Independent unions have limited memberships and limited goals. Their bargaining efforts are confined to convincing management of the rightfulness of their proposals for economic improvements. The arguments they use are based largely on comparisons within their own industry. The emphasis is on their role as an integral segment of the company in a continuing effort to assure success in a common endeavor.

To define precisely the philosophical difference between a union that confines its membership and its right of representation to employees of a particular company or a part of a company and a union that does not, may seem difficult at first blush, but the difference becomes increasingly apparent by an examination of both the characteristics and the practices of each.

The independent union cannot exist apart from the particular company whose employees it represents. Both in theory and in practice it complements the other two parts of the company—stockholders and management. These three working in harmony, although each has its own special interest, are more likely to achieve the goals of the company than if one of the parts is oriented toward goals that either are in conflict, or simply are not in communion, with those of the company. The nature of the national union, on the other hand, is to represent "labor" in the larger sense, transcending the employees of a particular company —thereby separating them from their normal relationship to the company; creating a gap that cannot be bridged.

Many observers have tried to understand and portray the nature and accomplishments, or lack of them, of independent unions. But, unless one has worked closely with these organizations over many years, has sat at the bargaining table, and has seen negotiating committees actually at work, it is difficult indeed, if not impossible, to present a true picture of the independent union. Furthermore, unless one has seen such groups during periods when they are not negotiating agreements, working in a hundred different ways to maintain their organizations' economic viability in the absence of compulsory union provisions in their agreements, their dedication to their task cannot be fully appreciated. Their problems may be legion; their solutions often seem inspiring.

No one ever has said, and no one should say, that an independent union must possess the same kind of strength, or use the same kind of weapons as the national unions. But this is far different from saying that they do not achieve the kind of results that the employees whom they represent want them to achieve. There is almost a mystique about how and why an independent union stays in existence in view of the incessant barrage of propaganda extolling the virtues of national unions. Admittedly, like other human institutions, some of them fall by the wayside. Where they do not survive, the reasons for their demise could encompass anything from lack of understanding of their limits by the leadership with a corresponding incapacity to utilize their strengths, to successful "take over" efforts by national unions.

Members of negotiating committees of independent unions are elected from among fellow employees and presumably do not possess the expertise necessary to field the arguments made by sophisticated management negotiators. Then why do they survive? Because there is an integrity on both sides that recognizes that bargaining *per se* is not the be all and end all of existence. Rather it is recognized as a forum that permits open and frank discussion of employer–employee misunderstandings—including a realistic look at prevailing wages, hours and working conditions in the industry—with a firm resolution at least to meet them through negotiations. Foolish beyond words is that management which does not value the opportunity to resolve differences directly with employee-elected representatives. As a further plus, participation in the decision-making process which constitutes bargaining has a salutary effect on responsible employee representatives. This is a by-product of independent union bargaining and a mighty precious one.

Local-level bargaining enables the employer and the employees' representatives to hammer out agreements that will be satisfactory to the employees, by virtue of their ratification, and suitable to the employer from the standpoint of carrying on the business of the company competitively *and without work stoppages.* The "hammering out" process may at times be (and, from the author's participation in it, has been) painful to the point of frustration; but better that the hammering be done *inside* the house than *at* the house.

Unless one has been present at the bargaining that ultimately results in agreement between the parties, no words can describe the feeling of fulfillment experienced when the handshake across the table coincides with the look of relief on the faces of everyone involved. The alternative to bargaining on the local level is power unions and all they imply; or a high degree of paternalism by the company. This latter approach hardly squares with today's emphasis on participatory democracy; nor was paternalism as practiced in the past ever a worthwhile substitute for negotiation. Negotiation is men acting freely. Paternalism is softened authoritarianism.

Robert S. Brod, a retired member of the JSTOA (an independent union of licensed officers employed aboard the American-flag vessels of Esso—now Exxon), and one who played an important role in its early years, recently wrote the association giving his views of local-level bargaining. These were based on his experiences as a member of the JSTOA executive committee and now from the perspective of a retiree:

> The best contracts are those which are in force for a long time. These should provide for a regular review and should be amended in the light of changing conditions.
>
> Since a viable and mutually satisfactory contract is the result of hard bargaining and compromise over a lengthy time span it follows that there were times and conditions when one or the other side benefited to a greater degree. Over the years this will average out.
>
> A contract is the sum of the above lengthy experiences; and since history has shown either or both sides to have made concessions, which in fact they later would have liked to withdraw or modify—it follows that a primary precaution is, do not ever terminate an existing contract with many years of amendments. This is especially true if the conditions are generally as good or better than the average in the industry.
>
> If, for example, there are somewhat better conditions prevailing in some parts of the industry and these conditions cannot be attained in your company, insist that the company justify their reasons for not meeting them. They may point out they have provisions in their agreement that other companies do not, and that these are more costly.
>
> They may, however, be amenable to granting other benefits, expanding or improving existing benefits. They may say "the time is not right"—"some other time." Do not be too quick to insist on a showdown. The company may, at the time, have internal reasons for not agreeing to a certain proposal which they cannot

divulge. In my long years of experience with this attitude, I found subsequently they often were justified.

And finally don't ask for the moon; do be realistic and flexible. Don't try or expect to get it all in one year—but at the same time if you believe you are right and have the facts (from comparison) to support your position, sit tight. You will win out in the end—and you will feel better for having stood your ground.[7]

When one has witnessed the intense interest of employee representatives in their task, and has seen them utilizing all the shadings and nuances of the bargaining process, only then, and at best intuitively, can the intimate relationship that prevails between the employees' and management's negotiating team be grasped. It is the power, persuasiveness and logic of the arguments presented, developed at times during bitter debates, that spell the success of local-level bargaining. This is especially true where representatives of the independent union effectively employ comparable data within the framework of their industry.

And by success is meant the benefit to the employees of continuous improvement in their economic situation without the loss of a single day's income because of a labor dispute; the advantage to the employer of being confident that he can keep his operation going 365 days a year, year in and year out, and remain competitive; and, of course, the gain to the general public in not having goods and services denied them by virtue of a work stoppage.

Critics of the independent union reach for all manner of "arguments" to denigrate it. They talk of the supposed weaknesses of its structure, its amateurish leadership, and its lack of bargaining strength. By bargaining strength they mean the use of sheer economic muscle. They fail to mention that most employers have matching economic muscle. It is true independent unions have a distaste for, if not a downright indifference to, economic warfare—the strike. They would prefer to make their progress by the more difficult route of continuous bargaining—finally to reach agreement. Only those who have participated in the bargaining process know how difficult this can be. Sheer endurance, both mental and emotional, many times provides the final answer—an agreement. Without this first-hand knowledge of the bargaining difficulties faced by independent unions, critics, nonetheless, with an invidious inference, frequently allege a too close relationship between the independent union and the employer. They seemingly see no inconsistency, however, in terming such a relationship "healthy" where national unions prevail.

These criticisms plus a host of other fanciful faults that fit their doctrinaire objection to it, constitute the arsenal of the denigrators. And while their views may influence the gullible, the simple fact is, they do not understand the philosophy of the independent union. The concept of an organic, living, and continuing institution, comprised of employees, management, and stockholders, termed collectively "the company," where bargaining is done within the institution, is totally foreign to their way of thinking.

It does not square with their "building block" beliefs. They cannot have any rapport with it emotionally, because they live in a world of "make believe," where a promise of pie in the sky is almost as real as the eating; where belief in conflict and the adversary concept leave little room for compromise, much less cooperation. They refuse to recognize that *man's liberties are protected by his obligations,* and that every human institution has and must have limitations; and that it is a mark of wisdom to be aware of this. Finally, their stubborn disbelief in the efficacy of the independent union even when faced with the facts of its economic, and other gains, makes the task of teaching them well nigh hopeless.

This recital of local-level bargaining therefore is not for them. Rather it is for the average man or woman who has enough common sense to know that no institution is perfect, but at least is sufficiently interested to learn about a kind of approach that has enabled *some* human beings to resolve *some* of their differences. Local-level bargaining promises no millennium, but neither does it encourage chaos.

There are countless examples of satisfactory employer–employee relations carried on year after year via independent unions in hundreds of corporations throughout the United States. The bargaining groups generally are small and since their bargaining rarely involves a work stoppage, there is little if any information about them in the public press. In the steel industry, just to cite one of many examples, there are independent unions in Armco and National Steel whose beginnings date to the nineteen-thirties. Efforts have been made by the Steel Workers Union (AFL–CIO) to take over these independent unions, but have not met with success. And while there have been several major steel strikes, there never has been a work stoppage involving the independent unions in Armco or National Steel.

To establish the validity and the value of independent unions one would have to probe deeply into their history. Even then, as will be noted from a perusal of the literature on independent unions, the information is spotty. In large measure it is prepared by third parties, based on discussions with employees and management, plus questionnaires. These hardly can be substituted for participation in the activity when making an evaluation of its merits.

The author for thirty-five years has been the adviser to several independent unions in the maritime industry. Membership in these separate unions has comprised both officer personnel and unlicensed seamen employed aboard the American-flag, deep-sea tankers of certain major oil companies—Exxon, Mobil, Texaco, Getty, and Cities Service, plus at least two non-oil companies.

The first chairman of the Maritime Commission, Joseph P. Kennedy, in November 1937 transmitted to the Congress *The Economic Survey of the American Merchant Marine.* In that survey it was stated, "Labor conditions in the American Merchant Marine are deplorable. Unless something is done to reduce interunion friction, to increase the efficiency of our crews, and to restore order and discipline upon our ships, all government efforts to develop a strong American fleet will be futile. A merchant marine built upon inadequate and unsatisfactory personnel is little better than no merchant marine at all." [8]

More than thirty-five years later, another chairman of the Maritime Commission, Helen Bentley, the first woman to hold that post, lashed out at a major national union for having engaged in a 47-day work stoppage on the West Coast that literally sabotaged, she said, two years of painstaking effort by the Maritime Commission to revitalize the American Merchant Marine and make it again attractive to American shippers. The occasion for Mrs. Bentley's remarks was a dinner given in her honor by the Council of Master Mariners of America at the New York Yacht Club in Manhattan, January 15, 1973.

Most of the independent unions in the tanker industry were formed during the tumultuous strike-ridden years 1937–1938. Their history has been related in some detail by the author during a drama-filled twenty-five-year period 1937–1962. In *Never Off Pay,* the beginnings, the battles, and the accomplishments of these groups have been documented in detail.[9]

In continuing the story of these organizations which are "alive and well" ten years later in an industry dominated by powerful national unions, it is not intended to make invidious comparisons with national unions, but rather to stress the virtue of pluralism in labor organization. In fairness to national unions representing seamen, it should be emphasized that these organizations have played a real role over the past forty years in the economic life of the average seaman. Traditionally, "going to sea" has been an uncertain experience. In years past "fly-by-night" shipowners in collusion with "crimp joint" operators and similar shady characters who "shipped" seamen, made a seaman's employment experience an unenviable one. Their plight was poignantly described in that part of *The Economic Survey of the American Merchant Marine* dealing with labor.[10] National seamen's unions have helped change this. Two types of control have brought this about. First, control of hiring, using for the most part the union hall as the place of employment, and shipping from there on a rotary basis; secondly, through control of welfare and pensions, made possible by employer contributions to the national unions.

By these controls national unions have secured for the seamen they represent a stability of employment that has revolutionized their former "casual labor" status. No longer can a seaman be sold to the highest bidder and later tossed on a human scrap pile when his usefulness allegedly has ended. The breed of shipowner who indulged in these callous tactics and who in large measure helped spawn the national unions, unfortunately, however, has not disappeared. He simply is marking time until he can begin again.

But not all shipowners are indifferent or callous toward seamen. There are companies, especially the international oil companies with substantial American-flag fleets, who have tried to project the image of a fair employer—and who have a sincere interest in the welfare of all their employees, including those at sea. Therefore, despite the national-union-dominated atmosphere, and the perennial sharp turnover in seagoing personnel, a large segment of seamen employed by these major oil companies aboard their vessels came to the conclusion long ago, and continue in the same conviction, that their best interests are served by bargaining at the local level.

The agreements they have negotiated have more than kept pace in wages, overtime and vacations with those negotiated by national seamen's unions. In addition ample fringe-benefit coverage while employed, and protection via substantial pensions during the twilight of their lives, exceed that provided by national unions for their members. Above all, these have been accomplished without work stoppages. This has meant continuous employment for the men who man the vessels and uninterrupted service by the vessels. If, therefore, the viability of bargaining on the local level can be demonstrated in an industry as volatile as the maritime industry, perhaps the nationwide advantages of local-level bargaining can better be understood.

NOTES

1. Hearings: Senate Committee on Education and Labor, S.1958, Washington, March 1934.
2. *Employee Representation Plans: A Study* (New York: National Industrial Conference Board, 1932).
3. National Labor Relations Act 8(2)
4. David J. Saposs (Chief Economist) and Elizabeth T. Bliss (Junior Economist), Division of Economic Research, National Labor Relations Board, "Current Anti-Labor Activities" (mimeographed), *Memorandum to Staff* (Washington, March 1938), p. 22.
5. *The American Can Case,* 13 NLRB 1252, 4LRRM 392 (1939).
6. Agreement, Ford Motor Company–United Auto Workers.
7. Letter, Robert S. Brod, retired member of Executive Committee Jersey Standard Tanker Officers Association, November 21, 1972.
8. United States Maritime Commission, November 10, 1937, *Economic Survey of the American Merchant Marine* (Washington: United States Government Printing Office, 1937), pp. 43, 44.
9. John J. Collins, *Never Off Pay* (New York: Fordham University Press, 1964).
10. United States Maritime Commission, *op. cit.*

1

Has Local-Level Bargaining Worked?

TO DETERMINE PRECISELY whether or not any human institution works is not the same as mixing two chemicals and being certain of the result. In human institutions, objectives must be known and then judgments made on the basis of the extent to which those judging believe the objectives have been realized.

Bargaining on the local level by independent unions involves the use of two primary yardsticks in deciding from a purely pragmatic standpoint whether or not it has worked. One, have the economic desires of the employees been reasonably realized, using as a guide their ratification of agreements negotiated by their elected representatives? Two, have these results been achieved without disturbing the stability of the economic institution of which they are an integral part? On both counts, based on the author's personal knowledge and involvement with this form of bargaining in the maritime industry, local-level bargaining may be said to have scored well. During the 35 years that independent unions have functioned in this industry they have not caused a single work stoppage; and, as will be detailed later, agreements which they have negotiated have been superior to those negotiated by national unions—if, in evaluating these agreements, total annual compensation is considered together with fringe benefits available both to employees and their families. Fringe benefits include retirement compensation. A quick comparison of those available to Texaco officers represented by the Texaco Tanker Officers Association with those available to officers represented by national unions establishes this superiority. (TABLES I–IV)

Companies in other industries bargaining on the local level presumably have met these tests of overall superiority in total compensation and, especially, continued stability in employer–employee relations—since where work stoppages do occur, they are quick to receive public notice; and there has been little of this.

TABLE I
TEXACO BENEFITS *UNAVAILABLE* TO NATIONALS*

Length of Service Increments (LOSI)

	Average Payments Monthly	Annually
Master	$150	$1,800
Chief Engineer	145	1,740
Chief Mate–First Assistant Engineer	115	1,380
Second Mate–Second Assistant Engineer	90	1,080
Third Mate–Third Assistant Engineer	85	1,020

Confidential Deferred Compensation Plan (CDCP)

	Annually
Master	$1,560
Chief Engineer	1,560
Chief Mate–First Assistant Engineer	840
Second Mate–Second Assistant Engineer	720
Third Mate–Third Assistant Engineer	600

Standby pay awaiting assignment

Standby pay is paid at the daily rate for each day the officer in Texaco is *available* for assignment following the completion of his paid leave. There can be no standby pay under national union contracts as officers upon termination of their vacation report to the union office and are not on pay while waiting to ship.

* Figures furnished by Texaco, Inc.

In 1936, Myron Taylor, Board Chairman of U. S. Steel Corporation, made a personal pact with John L. Lewis—then leader of the militant CIO—to recognize the United Steel Workers without benefit of a Labor Board-conducted election. Since that momentous decision there have been many steel strikes—some of them industry-wide, some of them wildcat. However, employees in at least two steel companies, Armco and National Steel, had formed independent unions during this period (1937–1943) and have successfully resisted periodic take-over attempts of the Steel Workers Union.[1] In Armco there have been four elections conducted by the National Labor Relations Board between the years 1944 and 1964. In each of these the Armco independent was the winner. In the last two they defeated the AFL–CIO Steelworkers by better than 3 to 1. A comparison of contracts negotiated by

TABLE II
PRESENT PAYMENTS AND BENEFITS *AFFECTED* BY THE 1973 WAGE INCREASE NEGOTIATED BY THE TEXACO TANKER OFFICERS ASSOCIATION WITH TEXACO*

	Texaco		Nationals
Savings Plan			
Monthly Company Contribution	yes		no
	from	*to*	
Master	$69.00	$75.00	0
Chief Engineer	66.00	72.00	0
Chief Mate–First Assistant Engineer	42.00	45.00	0
Second Mate–Second Assistant Engineer	39.00	39.00†	0
Third Mate–Third Assistant Engineer	33.00	36.00	0
Permanent and Total Disability	yes		no
Life Insurance	yes		no
Pension	yes		no
Extra Holiday	yes		no
Accident/Sickness Daily Payment	yes		no
Master	$82.78	$87.50	$7.00‡
Chief Engineer	79.49	83.97	7.00
Chief Mate–First Assistant Engineer	50.98	53.83	7.00
Second Mate–Second Assistant Engineer	44.84	47.37	7.00
Third Mate–Third Assistant Engineer	40.64	42.90	7.00

* Figures furnished by Texaco, Inc.
† Wage increase did not in this instance move these officers to next pay bracket necessary to effect an increase in company contribution to Savings Plan.
‡ $50 per week while sick.

the independent union in Armco with contracts bargained by the Steel Workers establishes the superiority of the former. Using the schedule of Sickness and Accident Weekly Benefits payable by the terms of the agreement between Armco and the independent union representing Armco employees and the industry-wide CIO Steelworkers agreement, the advantages to the Armco employees can readily be discerned. And this advantage will apply wherever wage payments are made. (TABLE V)

Furthermore, there never has been a work stoppage in the Armco plant at Middletown, Ohio, where the independent union

TABLE III
RETIREMENT INCOME
TEXACO VS. NATIONALS*

It is assumed that because of the manner that an officer in national unions accumulated credit for pension purposes that such officer will have worked *25 years* in order to qualify for his 20-year pension.

The Texaco officer receives full credit for each year of service. Therefore, this comparison is based on 25 years of actual service in Texaco.

	Pension[†]	Employees Savings Plan	Confidential Deferred Compensation Plan	Total
Nationals[†]				
Master	$ 826.52			$ 826.52
C/E	758.59			758.59
CM–1A/E	522.68			522.68
2M–2A/E	462.20			462.20
3M–3A/E	401.72			401.72
Texaco[‡]				
Master	$1,129.65	$313	$15	$1,457.65
C/E	1,084.91	259	15	1,358.91
CM–1A/E	664.50	213	9	886.50
2M–2A/E	589.63	170	8	767.63
3M–3A/E	532.49	112	5	649.49

* Figures furnished by Texaco, Inc.
† Based on wages effective 6/16/73.
‡ Based on wages effective 9/1/73.

is the bargaining representative. In their Ashland, Ohio plant where Armco employees are represented by the Steel Workers there have been 25 strikes in 17 years (1943–1961); some were general strikes, some were wildcat.[2]

Additional observations illustrating the advantages of contracts negotiated by the Armco independent union appear as follows in the *Key Contract Comparisons* study:

> During the seventeen years the Armco Employees Independent Federation has been bargaining agent here (Middletown, Ohio), the steel industry has been plagued with many bitter and costly CIO strikes. However, our Middletown plants have never been closed by a strike. No Armco employee has ever missed a payday, nor has the economic health of the community been impaired because Armco plants were shut down by a labor dispute. Our operations here have grown steadily and the number of employees

TABLE IV
ESTATE COMPARISONS TEXACO VS. NATIONALS*

Prior to Retirement

	Nationals	Texaco
Master		
Life Insurance	$20,000	$ 69,000
Employee Savings Plan (ESP)		65,430
Confidential Deferred Compensation Plan (CDCP)		3,177
TOTAL	$20,000	$137,607
C/E		
Life Insurance	$20,000	$ 66,000
ESP		54,180
CDCP		3,099
TOTAL	$20,000	$123,279
CM–1A/E		
Life Insurance	$20,000	$ 42,000
ESP		44,520
CDCP		1,980
TOTAL	$20,000	$ 88,500
2M–2A/E		
Life Insurance	$20,000	$ 39,000
ESP		35,640
CDCP		1,740
TOTAL	$20,000	$ 76,380
3M–3A/E		
Life Insurance	$20,000	$ 33,000
ESP		23,430
CDCP		1,110
TOTAL	$20,000	$ 57,540

* Figures furnished by Texaco, Inc.

has increased substantially. The hourly wage scale of our Middletown employees is higher than the scale in effect throughout the industry. Our insurance programs for employees are far more liberal than those of other steel companies.

TABLE V
ARMCO EMPLOYEES INDEPENDENT FEDERATION
VS.
CIO STEEL INDUSTRY CONTRACTS[3]

Sickness & Accident Weekly Benefit

Hourly Base Rate At Least	But Less Than	ARMCO-AEIF	Steel Industry-CIO	Advantage to ARMCO-AEIF
$2.10	$2.40	$60	$53–56	$4–7
2.40	2.88	65	56–59	6–9
2.88	3.36	70	59–62	8–11
3.36	3.84	75	65–68	7–10
3.84	4.32	75	68	7
4.32	4.80	75	68	7
4.80 or more		75	68	7

... On the basis of the $2,200 average loss (estimated by the press during the 116-day strike in 1959), Armco employees in the bargaining unit here earned some $16,000,000 during the strike period which they would have lost if they had been represented by the CIO. However, since their wages are higher, and they worked a great deal of overtime, their actual savings were considerably higher.[4]

Because of some blind spot in their intellectual outlook, many students of labor relations cannot conceive that the quiet and continuing existence of a relationship between management and employees, by its very quietness and continuity is an example of strength that no amount of designed discord and disorder can match. There is a dignity identified with the individual which some spokesmen for "labor" insist on submerging—to satisfy their "collectivist" approach to solving employee problems. Local-level bargaining tries to keep its ear attuned to the wishes of employees as a group, without sacrificing the sovereignty of the individual. This is not easy; but, generally speaking, the smaller the group, the greater the possibility of attaining that goal. The tragedy of the independent union and the local-level bargaining it reflects is the undeniable fact that its story is untold—at least nationally. And yet, in almost every company where independent unions function, they are like small choirs, singing their song of success, albeit with only their relatively tiny congregations listening. The broad channels of communication for good or for evil are reserved for the "big" and the "powerful"—especially if they are powerful enough to disturb the public order. It is the patient plodding, the unheralded prudence, and the ability—by the believers in local-level bargaining—to distinguish the possible from the desired, that has built a nationwide network of good will between management and employees. For this, society owes the participants in local-level bargaining a debt of gratitude which best can be paid by encouraging its growth.

THE LITERATURE OF LOCAL-LEVEL BARGAINING

Since the definition of local-level bargaining for this study is that which is done by independent unions, the literature with respect to this type of organization also will be limited to this concept. First it should be noted that the nature of the independent union does not lend itself to publicity, scholarly or otherwise. Its areas of activity are narrow; its agreements seldom pioneering in the sense that new wage patterns are set; they are rarely if ever on strike; and their political muscle is next to nil. Admittedly, they do not dominate the stage in the drama of collective bargaining; nor do they seek this dubious distinction. Some of these statements will provide critics of this form of organization with the kind of arguments they enjoy. It helps them to demean it. For example, they say the fact that strikes have been few and far between, if at all, is "proof" that the independent union has little or no strength. By strength they mean the liberal use of the bludgeon. Moral and intellectual strength to them are considered the weapons of paper tigers.

The literature on local-level bargaining has been written largely by academicians in the field of labor relations, not bargainers fresh from the negotiating arena. Leo Troy, Associate Professor at Rutgers University, has prepared several monographs dealing with the origins and operations of this particular form of labor organization and has made an evaluation of it. His articles have appeared in the *Journal of Political Economy*;[5] in the *Industrial and Labor Relations Review*;[6] and in a pamphlet published by the Institute of Management and Labor Relations at Rutgers University. He also has written an article for Industrial Relations Counselors, Inc., entitled "Management and the Local Independent Union."[7]

A somewhat more ambitious effort, at least in the sense that it appears in book form, is *America's Forgotten Labor Organization*[8] (A Survey of the Role of the Single Firm Independent Union in American Industry). Written by Arthur B. Shostak of the Department of Sociology, University of Pennsylvania, it was published in 1962 by the Industrial Relations Section of the Department of Economics, Princeton University.

There are other more modest efforts to describe the workings of independent unions. Some of these are related to special cases, confined either to one industry or to one company in an industry, or to several companies in a particular geographic area. For example, an article appears in the *Labor Law Journal* for September 1961 entitled "Independent Unions in the Gulf Coast Petroleum Refining Industry—The Esso Experience." [9] Earlier, Theodore Purcell, S.J., a sociologist, prepared two studies that were published by the Harvard University Press—one in 1953 entitled *The Worker Speaks His Mind on Company and Union*.[10] This included a history of the major independent union in the meat-packing industry. His other study, entitled *Blue Collar Man*,[11] was published in 1960 and seeks to compare an independent union with two rival locals.

Some twenty years ago, Jack Barbash, a prolific writer in the field of labor relations wrote *Unions and Telephones*.[12] This was a study of the reasons why independent unions in certain segments of the telephone industry banded together to form a national federation and subsequently affiliated with the Communications Workers of America (AFL–CIO).

The latest information on the number of independent unaffiliated unions and the total number of employees for whom they bargain is contained in a study prepared by the Division of Industrial Relations, U. S. Bureau of Labor Statistics, issued in November 1969. Two interesting statements appear in the Preface to this study which bear out this author's belief that local-level bargaining either is demeaned or forgotten:

> Despite determined competition from national unions, unaffiliated intrastate and single-employer unions continue to account for a small, relatively stable proportion of the membership in organized labor. However, the American labor movement today usually is defined to include the AFL–CIO and its affiliated unions and the national unions outside the federation. *The existence of local unaffiliated unions, more often than not, is overlooked entirely.*[13]

A further indication that the concept of local-level bargaining has suffered from the desire of Big Labor to eliminate this form of competition can be seen in another statement in the Bureau of Labor Statistics' study.

The eclipse of the small unaffiliated local unions, which once accounted for a relatively significant segment of organized labor in the United States, began with the passage of the National Labor Relations (Wagner) Act in 1935, and was hastened by the emergence and growth of strong national unions during World War II.[14]

It is interesting to note that with respect to publications such as Shostak's *America's Forgotten Labor Organization,* writers not having personal experiences with the operation of independent unions and especially not having participated in the bargaining process, must make judgments based on questionnaires and interviews with individuals in several of these organizations. These judgments, of course, by virtue of the nature of the sources of information lack a great deal as far as understanding how these organizations work.

Shostak divides independent unions into what he terms "weak unions" and "strong unions." He says, for example, weak independent unions generally are small and . . .

> most weak bargainers are formed to escape the organizing efforts of a national union. . . .
> A typical weak union in the sample had been formed in 1958 in opposition to the aggressive organizing tactics of the International Teamsters Union. The 16 lumberyard workers involved had been thoroughly frightened and antagonized when their spokesman received threatening phone calls late at night, had paint splattered on his home and car, found nails strewn in his driveway and was eventually forced to request police protection. The lumberyard employees pledged then to avoid the Teamsters at any cost, even when that meant the formation of a weak, passive union.[15]

Instead of praising the courage of the sixteen lumberyard employees in opposing the power and threats of the Teamsters, Shostak obviously considers the independent union as weak and passive—presumably because it had few members.

Indicating further his own opinion of the merits of the independent union, Shostak states:

> A union organized on the basis of rejection of the big unions faces two debilitating problems: self-imposed isolation from the main stream of the American labor movement, and the pressure to win immediate gains from the employer. An employer interested in such a weak union can trade immediate contract gains

for an "understanding" regarding the long-term division of authority in the shop.[16]

What is so meritorious in being in the "mainstream of the American Labor movement," Shostak does not reveal. Another of his negative references is a complaint from the president of a rural union of 65 lumber mill workers who stated, "One of our big problems is that there are no labor lawyers in the area." [17]

With respect to "strong unions" Shostak in his analysis indicates that one of the factors in determining the efficacy of what he deems a strong independent union is its concern with labor legislation and social reform.

> A plant-orientation and concentration on the employer are both supplemented by union concern with area or industry labor standards, labor legislation, and social reform. This concern helps liberalize the independent union's characteristically conservative ideology at the same time that it challenges the notion that big unions and big government are everywhere conspiring against these unions. The strong union's comparatively large size and urban location weaken its commitment to the notion of smallness as a virtue, and may even encourage new interest in affiliation as a means of augmenting strength.[18]

In his concluding paragraph, Shostak seems sorry for the strong independent union because, while it has merit, its difficulty in publicizing its role does not enable it to grow in the manner in which he believes it should.

> Theoretically, such a strong independent union should prove a valid alternative for workers unimpressed with the international unions and with the weak single-firm unions. But an alternative must be known to decision-makers if they are to take it into account and this union is not known to the American working man. Paradoxically, this strong effective form of the single firm union is even more obscure than the weak form. It has figuratively had to use a hand press and megaphone to do a publicity job that demands the equivalent of a printing factory and many loudspeakers.[19]

Professor Troy appears to have a better understanding of the role of the independent union. In his evaluation he states:

> Besides full disclosure, other important elements have contributed, and can be expected to contribute, to a durable independent relationship. One is positive acceptance and support by management of local independent dealings. Top management policy regarding

this issue, imperfectly understood, coupled with insincere acceptance of the local independent by lower management will undermine the relationship. Another is management's recognition and acceptance of the fact that its relationship with the independent can change, especially in terms of the union's assertiveness. The union's effectiveness, being based on the employees' interests, is not a factor management can manufacture. Surely, however, if management functions effectively and openly, the union's leaders and members will find enough interest in their organization to desire its survival.[20]

In his prognosis he states:

Transfer of allegiance from independent unions to affiliated unions, and in some cases, back again to independent unions, will continue to occur as in the past.[21]

... Offsetting the tendencies for affiliation is the fact that localized bargaining is still the characteristic scope of labor relations in America and since the local independent engages only in such bargaining, it should have a durable future. In addition, there are often divisive forces within national unions and these can, and do, give rise to new independent unions. Finally, public policy, which provides for employee's free choice of bargaining representatives, will continue to provide support for this type of management–union relationship.[22]

These sketchy accounts can hardly tell the complete story of what the independent union has accomplished, both in the economics of bargaining—wages, overtime, and vacations—as well as the employment stability that it has encouraged. It is an historical fact however that in the highly volatile maritime industry during the years 1937–1973, employees, management, stockholders, and the general public have benefited from the local-level bargaining that has taken place in this industry. It is therefore on this industry that this study of local-level bargaining is largely focused.

Most Americans are said to be pragmatic. Assuming this to be so, how does bargaining on the local level work out in practice in the maritime industry? Are the accomplishments of independent unions in the maritime industry comparable with those of national unions—in wages, overtime, vacations, working conditions, and fringe benefits? At the outset it must be pointed out that in this industry it is especially difficult to make comparisons in such fringe benefit areas as pensions, welfare and *availability compensation*. The reason for this is because rules for eligibility for pensions and welfare under national union agreements are determined by the unions via negotiations with those employers who bargain with them. Most shipping companies long ago capitulated to the demands of national unions that fringe benefits be predicated on what so many cents—or later, so many dollars—per day, per man contributed to a fund by the employer could purchase.[23] (Later the concept was reversed and certain fixed benefits were negotiated —then the amounts necessary to provide these had to be determined.) National unions also bargained rules for shipping that are in the interest of the union and defy comparison with conditions and pay prevalent for officers represented by independent unions.

For example, an extremely important benefit available only to licensed officers represented by independent unions is the guarantee that at the conclusion of their vacation (or paid leave as it is more frequently termed) the officer remains on pay while awaiting assignment to a vessel. In other words he is "never off pay"—unless he elects to take a leave of absence for personal reasons. In the 1970 Exxon agreement (and this was a continuation of what previous agreements provided in this area) the clause providing this financial protection reads:

> Officers upon reporting from paid leave as instructed will be considered on active duty and will receive normal rate of pay (base pay plus seniority pay) according to seniority rating with the company plus full room and subsistence until assigned to a vessel.[24]

In practice an officer upon the termination of his paid leave frequently has been on "standby," awaiting assignment to a vessel, for several days. During this time he receives his regular rate of pay plus room and subsistence allowance.

A chief officer with ten years service as an officer in Exxon earned $65.43 per day under the terms of the 1970 agreement. The room and subsistence allowance was $21 per day.[25] Officers may remain home until notice of assignment to a vessel. By adding, therefore, the $21 to the daily rate of pay—$65.43—the officer under the terms of the 1970 Exxon agreement received $86.43 for each day he was waiting for an assignment. In addition, by the terms of the 1970 Exxon agreement his days of waiting assignment to a vessel were "active duty days." For each day of active duty he earned one-half-day of paid leave, or vacation. Thus if the chief mate referred to above was not assigned to a vessel until four days after his paid leave ended, he would have been compensated in the amount of $345.72. He also would have earned two days of paid leave.

While this is a costly arrangement for the company there is a distinct benefit to them in that the agreement gives the company the right to require the officer to report to active duty ten days before completion of his earned paid leave. Thus in exchange for a guarantee that the officer will be on pay with room and subsistence at the conclusion of his paid leave, while awaiting assignment, the company, if they need him, may shorten his paid leave by as many as ten days. (He is entitled to this leave later—unless he wishes to take the pay in lieu of the leave.) This gives the company the flexibility which they say they must have to operate their fleet efficiently.

It is difficult to compare this costly arrangement with what prevails under national union agreements. According to the terms of the International Organization of Masters, Mates and Pilots Agreement,

> Masters or Chief Officers who have accumulated one hundred eighty (180) days' employment aboard a vessel shall be relieved by the company upon the conclusion of the voyage in which the one hundred and eighty (180) day period occurs.[26]

Nowhere in the agreement of the national union is there mention of, or provision for, payment to an officer who is awaiting an assignment following his vacation. As a matter of fact an officer below the rank of chief officer, shipping as he must "Off the Board," rarely finds it possible to continue employment on the same vessel or even with the same company at the conclusion of his vacation. Furthermore, he is required by the National Union Agreement to

> take all of his earned vacation *plus* an additional period of time off *without pay,* which shall be equivalent to one-half of such period of earned vacation, before he can be re-employed.[27]

This situation alone clearly points up how different the philosophy of the national union is from that of the independent union; and this difference is predicated on control of hiring.

In respect to what is available in the form of health care, insurance, and pensions for members of a national union, the determination is almost entirely in the hands of the union. The monies to accomplish these goals are assessed against those shipping companies which bargain with the national unions. It is distinctly to the advantage of the leadership of the national union that its role in determining who gets what be paramount—since, if the average union member believes the medical, dental, or pension benefits he receives are union-generated and -controlled, the union's stature is enhanced. The latitude to select certain benefits, such as eyeglasses or dental work, both of which are of primary importance to the individual seaman, improves the prestige of the union even further. That he receives only $50 a week sick-leave reimbursement should he be off the vessel because of illness is soft-pedaled by national unions.

In the major oil companies, benefits long have been a part of the companies' employee-relations philosophy. Although there is bargaining with respect to benefits, the company—unless it is bargaining with a national union in the maritime industry—never gives to the union the administration of its pension and welfare programs. It consistently refuses to contribute to a welfare fund from which benefits can be doled out to the membership by the union. It is difficult, therefore, to compare benefits under these two distinctly different systems of providing them.

How, for example, can one compare the 26 weeks of full pay ($458 per week) while sick, plus 26 weeks of half pay if still ill, for a ten-year (officer service) chief officer in Exxon,[28] with the $50 a week paid from the welfare fund by a national union to their members, regardless of their normal earnings or length of service? [29] The gap is enormous. On the other hand, a chief officer under a national-union agreement could receive dental care,[30] whereas the hospital–medical–surgical plan applicable to a chief officer in Exxon does not include dental care.

Considered from the standpoint of cost to the company and the overall protection to the officer and his family, the Exxon benefits far exceed those available to an officer under their national-union welfare plan. Apart from the example of payments made to the individual while sick or otherwise incapacitated, Exxon's benefits are notable in the area of family protection, disability income, family adjustment insurance, and hospital–medical–surgical coverage.[31] Only in respect to the last category does the employee contribute a portion of the cost. Essentially the same kind of coverage in fringe benefits blankets licensed officers in Texaco, Getty, Mobil, and Cities Service, where independent unions are the bargaining representatives.

In the matter of pensions the yardstick for comparing this particular fringe benefit is more precise—at least with respect to the separately negotiated seagoing pension supplement. This was especially true when national unions finally negotiated an any-age pension that provided a minimum of $325 per month after 20 years of union-covered employment.[32] Here, as will be noted from the bargaining history of the independent unions on this issue, there was difficulty at first. This difficulty existed because of a differing attitude toward the part pensions play in the working career of the average employee. The position taken by management in major oil companies has been that the normal retirement age is 65—not retirement after 20 years' service regardless of age. And, although the basic company pension predicated on age, wage, and service does provide a substantial retirement income for the career employee, most major oil companies finally were persuaded to negotiate a competitive 20-year retirement plan for their seagoing employees *in addition to the company-wide career pension plan.*

The day-to-day bargaining in 1967–1968 on this special seagoing pension for licensed officers employed aboard the American-flag tankers of Mobil is a vivid illustration of the patience and persistence of the independent union that had represented these officers since 1937. This account, as later described, will more clearly reveal the validity of the bargaining that took place in an extremely difficult and delicate area—pensions.

From the long-range view, however, the highlights that marked improvements in wages, vacations, and overtime negotiated by independent unions bring into even sharper focus the progress made in these basic areas in this thirty-five-year period.

1937 VERSUS 1973—THE GENERATION GAP

A commonplace topic today is the generation gap which people define differently. Some say it constitutes a complete lack in communication between two groups separated by more than just years. Others say the electronic age, the mass media, the new permissiveness account for the difficulty in establishing dialogue between the generations. It may be all and then again it may be none of these, but rather just an expression for a phenomenon that always has existed. Without question there are real changes that separate the generations. These may be economic, social, or cultural, or all three, and they are clearly identifiable. Nowhere is this more discernible than in the wage patterns established over the course of at least one generation. The Mobil case is not unique but there is sufficiently precise information available to document the economic changes that have occurred within a single group of employees in one company over a span of thirty-five years.

Begun in 1937 by Fred Hansen, Chief Engineer, and Frank Girardeau, Chief Mate, of the s.s. *Magnolia,* an American-flag vessel of the then Socony Vacuum Oil Company, the Socony Vacuum Tanker Officers Association (since renamed the Mobil Tanker Officers Association) was readily endorsed by their fellow-officers in the fleet with such encouraging letters as the following:

s. s. *Rochester*
New York, New York
September 20, 1937

Dear Sir:

We received letters aboard our ship, a week ago, from Mr. F. N. Hansen, and Mr. F. C. Girardeau, proposing an independent organization of officers, of the Socony Tankers.

We have been thinking along the same line for some time, and are pleased that someone has taken the initiative.

The formation of such an organization, before the National Labor Board vote is taken, is approved by us and we will give it our support.

We are mailing one letter, as the independent organization of officers of the Socony tankers is freely approved by each of the undersigned.

S. SORENSEN, *Master*	H. W. PINKHAM, *Chief Engineer*
S. P. LETH, *1st Mate*	M. J. CULLINANE, *1st Asst. Eng'r.*
V. H. WEAVER, *3rd Mate*	WM. R. WOLFE, *2nd Asst. Eng'r.*
	D. R. FLYNN, *3rd Asst. Eng'r.*[33]

This enthusiasm for an organization which they alone would control was understandable in light of what the first chairman of the U. S. Maritime Commission, Joseph P. Kennedy, called the deplorable labor conditions of the American Merchant Marine where the picket line had been substituted for the conference table.

It was equally understandable that the executive committee of the association was elated with, and the membership overwhelmingly approved, the first agreement with the company negotiated in January 1938. As the report of the executive committee later described it: "When, therefore, this agreement was presented to the members, calling for a 7½ per cent increase in pay, increases in vacation, overtime and night relief in New York and New England ports, the members rushed to signify their approval." [34]

The years 1937 and 1938 were depression years, which also might have accounted for the warm reception accorded this first step in what was to become a long and successful history in bargaining between the association and the company. The second agreement negotiated in 1939 achieved a further improvement in wages and overtime.

A quick comparison of these 1939 wages, overtime, and vacations (which had been increased over what prevailed in 1938) with those negotiated in January 1973, describes what has happened in this time-span.[35]

The wages of a chief mate as they appeared in the 1939 agreement were $245 per month; the wages of a chief mate by the terms of the 1973 agreement are $1483.44 per month. The overtime rate by the terms of the 1939 agreement was $1.00 per hour; in the 1973 agreement, it is $12.12 per hour. In 1939, overtime was not paid for work performed or watches stood on Saturdays, Sundays, and holidays. In 1973, overtime for these days is payable whether a ship is at sea or in port. Since the watchstanding officers work a 56-hour week, they are guaranteed 16 hours of overtime for each weekend, or a minimum of 70 hours a month. At the rate of $12.12 per hour, this will add approximately $850 per month to a chief mate's base wage while assigned to a vessel. There also is overtime for work in excess of 8 hours in any day.[36]

A further revealing picture of a substantial monetary benefit negotiated by the various independent unions in the maritime industry, including Mobil, is the following schedule of additional compensation for length of service calculated on a career basis. (TABLES VI, VII) If compound interest were added to these amounts (presuming the individual deposited this "extra income" in a savings bank), the totals would be considerably greater. Similar formulas for length of service compensation prevail in other major oil companies with deep-sea fleets, where bargaining is done via independent unions. There is no additional remuneration for length of service in national union agreements. This is understandable because they are more interested in tying the individual to the *union* and they do not encourage him to remain continuously employed by a particular company.

The 1939 Mobil agreement provided for an annual vacation of 21 days. By the terms of the 1973 agreement, vacations—or paid leave, as it is now termed—are 16 days of paid leave for each 30 worked or approximately *128 days per year*. Mention is not made of the substantial improvements in pensions and other fringe bene-

TABLE VI
CHIEF MATE AND FIRST ASSISTANT ENGINEER
CUMULATIVE LENGTH OF SERVICE INCREASE IN EARNINGS*

After Years of Service	Texaco	Humble & Mobil
1	$ 120	$ —
3	360	216
5	1,800	792
10	5,700	2,952
15	11,100	6,912
20	18,080	12,672
25	26,600	20,032
30	36,700	29,032
35	48,300	38,032

* Figures supplied by Texaco's Marine Department during 1972 negotiations with the TTOA.

TABLE VII
SECOND MATE—SECOND ASSISTANT ENGINEER
CUMULATIVE LENGTH OF SERVICE INCREASE IN EARNINGS

After Years of Service	Texaco	Humble	Mobil
3	$ —	$ 216	$ 216
5	1,800	792	792
10	5,700	2,952	2,952
15	11,100	6,912	6,912
20	17,100	12,672	12,672
25	23,100	20,032	19,872
30	29,100	29,032	27,072
35	35,100	38,032	34,272

fits that have taken place in the intervening years, nor of working conditions which also changed markedly for the better. Yet based on membership reaction as reflected by balloting conducted by the American Arbitration Association, the 1973 agreement was not that impressive.[37] It received just barely enough votes to constitute the majority necessary for ratification. It hardly would be fair, however, to categorize current employee attitudes as reflecting a certain cynicism, solely on the strength of this close vote. Essentially this same group of officers in 1970 understandably approved overwhelmingly an agreement that provided the largest wage and overtime increase ever negotiated to be spread over a three-year period.[38] It was difficult for the association to make the same economic advance in 1973 as had been made in 1970, and the members' disappointment was reflected in their vote.*

Should the reader be concerned for Mobil's economic existence in the light of these substantial changes in compensation, mention should be made that during this period Mobil's ships have become larger (in many cases at least three times larger in carrying capacity) and faster; and the turnaround time for both loading and discharging has markedly improved, and, of course, tanker rates are sharply higher. This latter has been especially true during periods of crisis such as the volatile Middle East situation including the closing of the Suez Canal.

The construction of the Colonial Pipe Line in 1962 cut sharply into East Coast tanker transportation causing in part the substantial reduction in Mobil's American-flag fleet, so that today, in tonnage, Mobil's nine-ship, American-flag fleet does not carry the volume their forty-ship fleet carried in 1937. However, the current energy crunch, plus possible legislation regarding foreign-flag imports and dollar devaluation, could result in a new building program for American-flag vessels.

There is a tendency to generalize, whether in our evaluation of employees of the 'seventies and their attitude toward work, or in reaching conclusions as to the "why" of their specific actions. When one probes beneath the surface, however, we find the same basic human nature responding to the normal desires of employees for security, recognition, and equitable treatment. Where employees believe that company concern for any of these is lacking, be it in 1937 or 1973, they will so indicate by their vote, or in whatever manner they wish to express their disapproval. This is democracy in practice. To those involved in local-level bargaining, democracy represents difficulties—but never doubts—as to its efficacy.

This partial picture of some wage, overtime, and vacation changes over 35 years—all negotiated through local-level bargaining between Mobil and the independent union representing their licensed officers—should be convincing proof that an independent union is effective for those it represents. The intimate participation of the membership in local-level bargaining by making meaningful decisions is democracy at work.

---

* Confirming this changing employee reaction was the solid two-to-one vote ratifying the 1974 Mobil agreement.

That all this has been accomplished without loss of pay to the officers or interruption in the continuous operations of the company's vessels over this 35-year period (and this is equally true where independent unions exist elsewhere in this industry), is an added dividend. Over and beyond these direct benefits, the stability that bargaining on the local level has contributed to the American Merchant Marine is a plus for the public, on which a price cannot readily be set.

To put the finishing touches on this chapter as well as to enjoy talking to an old friend whose well of wisdom never ran dry, the author had visited the late Fred Hansen and his devoted wife where they lived in retirement in Jacksonville, Florida. Hansen was chief engineer on Mobil's (then Socony Vacumn's) s.s. *Magnolia* in 1937 when the CIO was making its successful drive to organize all American seamen, both licensed and unlicensed. His interest in local-level bargaining never waned.

His eyes lighted up as he reminisced, and in a vibrant voice reviewed his role in the formation of the first of several independent unions among licensed officers on tankers. At the author's request, he embodied the reasons for the action he took in 1937 in a letter:

> During the great depression of the early thirties, the officers of the Socony fleet suffered perhaps less than those in many other companies. The "share the work" plan was strictly but fairly applied by the company. The subsequent loss of earning power caused some hardship in individual cases, but by and large—with few men losing their jobs, conditions improving, wages and fringe benefits back—the officers of the Socony fleet, myself included, reached 1936–1937 in a good frame of mind in regard to our employment. Our wages, hours, working conditions, and steady employment were well ahead of those prevailing in other fleets which were controlled by national unions. I must say here that the conditions we had in Socony at the time were not due to any effort on our part other than that of doing the job for which we were paid—in a reasonably good and intelligent manner. The conditions were due solely to policies laid down by management. It must be supposed also that such policies were thought by management to be those best suited for the successful pursuit of the company's business. At any rate, the policies produced what in my opinion are most valuable assets—namely, loyalty and opportunity for pride in accomplishment by the individual. . . .
>
> Now, around this time, 1937 or a little before, the existing marine crew unions staged an intensive organizing campaign and

the various deck and engineer officers unions followed shortly after. The idea was—first, organize the crews in a certain company's fleet. Next, have these crewmen pressure the officers in various ways into joining one of their affiliated officers unions. This led to disagreeable conditions and incidents on many ships during the organizing campaign. Truth to tell but few of the incidents happened on Socony ships. Although the rapidly rising National Maritime Union (CIO) became the crew's union, the majority of the crew were not overly receptive to the eloquent soap-box oratory of the organizers; and secondly, the crew-officer relationship in the Socony fleet was very good.

However, the organizing campaign mentioned above was sufficient to alert myself and many other officers to the fact that, unless we took some action to protect the conditions under which we were working, we would in time be forced to join a union which would lower our standard of working conditions and wages, and also destroy the continuity of our employment with strikes, etc.

By inquiring correspondence and oral discussion when possible (the fleet at the time was spread over the world), it was found that there was a strong desire among the officers to "do something" in the direction indicated. It also was abundantly clear from these discussions or contacts that protection was not the only subject of which the men were thinking. They, as I myself, had in the back of their minds the idea that no matter how well the company treated the personnel afloat—we should have some say in matters affecting our daily living and working conditions. Also, it was thought desirable to have some means for handling or resolving grievances for the individual officer as well as those affecting the officer personnel collectively. . . . With this fairly concrete information to hand, a nucleus of officers, myself included, started energetically in pursuit of a solution to the problem. . . .

As before mentioned, the Socony officers were a fairly happy crowd and conditions were good in the ships before we formed our own union. But after the first agreement had been signed with the company there was a new and better feeling on the part of the officers. It could be said also that there was a new feeling in management.

The worry of the officers about having to join a union—not of their choice—was gone. And for the company the uncertainty of continuous operation had also largely disappeared—placing them in a better position for planning. Annual bargaining with the company by member-elected, unpaid representatives was provided for—enabling both the company and the officers to adjust to changing conditions and also to help bring about new conditions without at the same time adversely affecting the company's *com-*

petitive position. Individual grievances now could be settled by representation without jeopardy or fear to any individual.

So after all this longwinded writing, I will answer your initial question: I knew I wanted something to protect and improve our conditions as outlined above. I didn't know exactly what that "something" was until I had been working at it for some time, and THEN I saw clearly that what I wanted was—AN INDEPENDENT UNION! [39]

NOTES

1. National Labor Relations Board, *Decisions and Orders.*
2. Armco Steel Corporation, *Key Contract Comparisons (revised–1964)* Armco Employees Independent Federation *vs* CIO Steel Industry Contracts (Middletown, Ohio: Armco Steel Corporation, Armco Division, 1964), p. 9.
3. *Ibid.*
4. *Ibid.,* p. 8.
5. Leo Troy, "Local Independent and National Unions: Competitive Labor Organizations," *Journal of Political Economy,* 68, (1960), 499–502.
6. Troy, "Local Independent Unions and the American Labor Movement," *Industrial and Labor Relations Review,* 14 (1961), 331–349.
7. Leo Troy, "Management and the Local Independent Union," *Industrial Relations Memo No. 145,* Industrial Relations Counselors, Inc.
8. Arthur B. Shostak, *America's Forgotten Labor Organization,* Industrial Relations Section, Department of Economics, Princeton University, 1962.
9. F. Ray Marshall, "Independent Unions in the Gulf Coast Petroleum Refining Industry—The Esso Experience," *Labor Law Journal* (September 1961), 823–840.
10. Theodore V. Purcell, S.J., *The Worker Speaks his Mind on Company and Union* (Cambridge: Harvard University Press, 1953).
11. Purcell, *Blue Collar Man* (Cambridge: Harvard University Press, 1960).
12. Jack Barbash, *Unions and Telephones* (New York: Harper, 1952).
13. U.S. Department of Labor, Bureau of Labor Statistics, Bulletin No. 1640, *Unaffiliated Intrastate and Single Employer Unions–1967,* U.S. Government Printing Office, Washington, D.C., November, 1969. Emphasis added.
14. *Ibid.*
15. Shostak, *op. cit.,* pp. 29, 30.
16. *Ibid.* p. 30.
17. *Ibid.,* p. 30.
18. *Ibid.,* p. 52.
19. *Ibid.*
20. Troy, "Management and the Local Independent Union," pp. 54, 55.
21. *Ibid.*
22. *Ibid.*
23. Masters, Mates and Pilots (Atlantic and Gulf Districts), *Pension,* New York, no imprint. Marine Engineers' Beneficial Association, *MEBA Pension Trust Regulations,* effective January 1, 1956, New York, no imprint.
24. Agreement, Marine Department, Humble Oil and Refining Company and Jersey Standard Tanker Officers Association, March 13, 1970.

25. *Ibid.*
26. Masters, Mates and Pilots, ILA/AFL–CIO, Master Collective Bargaining Agreement, June 16, 1972, New York.
27. *Ibid.* Emphasis added.
28. Humble Oil & Refining Company, *A Guide to Your Employee Benefits,* June, 1972, p. 5.
29. Note 26.
30. *Ibid.*
31. Humble Oil and Refining Company, *A Guide to Your Employee Benefits,* pp. 1–43.
32. Masters, Mates and Pilots, Pension Agreement.
33. Socony Vacuum Tanker Officers Association, *Report* of the Executive Committee, 1937–41 (New York, 1941). Letter, September 20, 1937, pp. 6, 7.
34. *Ibid.*, pp. 16, 17.
35. SVTOA–Socony Vacuum Oil Company, Agreement, January 1, 1940; MTOA–Mobil Oil Company, Agreement, January 1, 1973.
36. *Ibid.*
37. Certification of Results, Ratification Ballot, American Arbitration Association, February 28, 1973.
38. Certification of Results, Ratification Ballot, American Arbitration Association, March 9, 1970.
39. Letter, Fred N. Hansen, January 25, 1973.

2

Bargaining on Pensions— The Mobil Approach

SOME NOTION OF THE DIFFICULTIES bargaining on the local level presents may be had from examining the on-going story and summaries of negotiations by several independent unions. The information relating to these negotiations is from the files of these independent unions, plus some interpolation by the author who was an "observer-participant" in all negotiations. In accordance with the Constitution and By-Laws of these organizations, membership ratification of agreements negotiated by the elected bargaining committees and management is necessary before the agreements can become effective. This has to be accomplished by mail since the members are at work on ships. Only in this way could the full story of the actual negotiations have been told. The process, though involved, becomes valuable for the scholar, since the necessity to reduce the bargaining story to the written word assures greater accuracy.

The negotiations to secure a special seagoing retirement plan are but a chapter in the history of local-level bargaining in the maritime industry, but are particularly illustrative of both its difficulties and its successes. Early retirement had been a primary objective of seagoing officers for years. It was when it became reachable that it became truly thorny. It was one of the most difficult issues faced by independent unions of seamen in the 'sixties. To understand the almost universal desire among seamen for early retirement requires a reasonable knowledge of the maritime industry. Going to sea under the best of conditions is difficult. Home life is impossible except for those brief periods when a ship is in port (and only when that port is the one where the officer lives), and during periods of paid leave (vacation). Even in the days of clipper ships, sea captains, once they had made a few successful voyages, often of long duration, were able to build their homes along the shores of New England and retire. And, while sailing, families often were welcomed as passengers, so that the psychological burden of being away from home was lightened. Today, most major oil companies with foreign-flag fleets provide quarters for officers' wives where the vessel trades away from the home port for long periods. Only one American-flag tanker operator, Cities Service, provides this convenience.

The adventure and romance of going to sea therefore must be seasoned, and seasoned well, with rewards, and money is not the only reward. Paid leave or extended vacations during a seaman's working life and early retirement to enable him to spend a reasonable portion of his remaining life ashore have been perennial goals, especially of independent unions. A revolutionary breakthrough in extended vacations had been bargained by the Jersey Standard Tanker Officers Association in 1946.[1] Negotiated with Esso (now Exxon) the JSTOA had, on a "trade off" basis, secured a formula for vacation—paid leave—of one day of paid leave for each three days of active duty. This guaranteed each officer 92 days of time off with pay in each year. The agreement became the talk of the industry and soon was followed by similar agreements negotiated between other major oil companies and the independent unions representing their seagoing personnel. In later years further advances were made in this area and national unions ultimately negotiated identical (as far as the number of days) paid leave, or vacation, arrangements for those whom they represented. By 1973 practically all unions representing seamen bargained vacations, or paid leave, of 16 days for each 30 worked.

Early retirement with pay was a different matter and proved to be more difficult to achieve. National unions of seamen had nothing in the way of retirement pay until the late 1950s. Many shipping companies operate in the economic climate of feast or famine. Until the national unions prodded them they did nothing to enable their seagoing officers to retire with a livable pension. Finally a beginning was made. Through a negotiated system of employer contributions on a per-man, per-day basis, national unions built up substantial sums toward pensions and welfare. The distribution of these monies, although nominally done by a joint employer–union arrangement, in practice became a powerful weapon both for organization purposes and for keeping the union members docile and controlled, since the actual doling-out of these benefits was done by the union.

When company contributions began, they were 25 *cents* per-day, per-man.[2] In 1973 contributions were in excess of 25 *dollars* per-man, per-day. By the mid-nineteen-sixties sufficient monies had been contributed—and more would be bargained—to provide those officers sailing on national-union-controlled ships with a lifetime minimum pension of $325 per month after 20 years of sea service, regardless of their age. In one of the negotiations that took place during this period national unions directed that a 6 per cent wage increase they bargained should enrich the pension and welfare account to provide for a larger pension. The entire industry was caught up with this pension phenomenon. Unions representing unlicensed seamen also had negotiated similar early-retirement plans. The same basic formula—a lifetime pension after 20 years of sea service—was used but with a smaller retirement income ($250 per month).

Since pensions negotiated by national unions, at least in the beginning, were not funded but were on a "pay as you go" basis, there was doubt in some quarters regarding their financial stability. On the other hand, the sharp turnover in the maritime industry worked in favor of financing pensions since hundreds, even thousands, of individuals were employed for short periods of time and never could qualify for a pension. Nevertheless, the employer was required to contribute the negotiated amounts each day for each seaman. Insurance experts know how much income for pension purposes can be generated in a short time under this arrangement. Despite the income advantages to the pension plans of rapid turn-over among seamen, national union pension plans were not always trouble-free. Among the reasons for this financial plight was the lay-up and sale of large numbers of ships, especially passenger liners. These latter vessels had upwards of 700 seagoing berths per ship. Their loss from the standpoint of pension contributions on a per-man, per-day basis was substantial; meanwhile payments to retirees had to continue.

Officers employed by major oil companies on their American-flag vessels and represented by independent unions were well aware of this attractive early retirement now available to members of national unions—and they wanted their unions to negotiate similar plans to enable them to retire after 20 years of seagoing service. This posed a serious problem for both management and the independent union in those several companies—i.e., Esso, Mobil, Texaco, Getty, and Cities Service. The reason the problem was serious and seemed for a while almost impossible of solution, was because the major oil companies already had a range of benefit plans which applied uniformly to all its employees—shore-based and seagoing. For a handful of employees (the seagoing group is a tiny fraction of the total number of employees in any of the major oil companies) to cause the company to change its pension-plan philosophy—to say nothing of the amount of money involved—was a David *versus* Goliath contest. The company pension plan (and this was true of all the oil companies) was predicated on years of service plus earnings, until the normal retirement age of 65. The independent union's proposal (each organization bargained separately) required that an employee work 20 years and then be permitted to retire, regardless of age, and receive a minimum $325 per month pension as had been bargained by national unions. When first presented to the several companies it was rejected out of hand.

Each of the companies argued that they offered their employees a career. Their pension philosophy and formula were based on employees' receiving pensions directly related to their earnings and their length of service in the company—to begin at age 65 or, under certain circumstances, at an earlier date subject to a discount. In no case could an employee retire prior to age 55. Employees also had "vesting rights," which meant that anyone who terminated his employment with the company before his normal retirement date could put aside (until the normal retirement date) whatever pension had been generated by his and the company's contributions while he had been employed. Also each of these companies had instituted "Savings" or "Thrift" plans which enabled the employees to build up nesteggs through a combination of their participation and the matching contributions of the company. Some of these nesteggs grew to sizable proportions. It was the company's intention, or at least hope, that these monies (i.e., "Savings" and "Thrift" funds), if left relatively undisturbed throughout an employee's working life in the company, could supplement whatever pension had been earned; so that these amounts, together with Social Security, would give every employee a livable retirement income.

In the light of what the parent petroleum companies considered generous and reasonably flexible retirement plans, the marine managements of these companies found themselves facing a stone wall of opposition from the benefit plan specialists in their own company. It always has been difficult for shoreside management to understand why things have to be different for their seagoing employees; and years of "educating" them in the legitimate differences has not seen too many of them graduating with honors.

One has to be intimately associated with seagoing personnel—either by having gone to sea or by having worked closely with seamen for years—to understand and appreciate their outlook and their desires. This communication gap between shoreside and seagoing personnel made the job of these independent unions representing seamen extremely difficult since now they were bargaining in a very delicate area—one near and dear to the hearts of fringe-benefit experts who had built their system of "employee protection" to cover all facets of all situations shoreside employees and their families might face throughout their employment career, in sickness, in retirement, and at death. And they were proud of the job they had done vis-à-vis other companies, and well they might be. Furthermore, the astronomical costs (so the companies argued) of putting a 20-year retirement plan "on top" of the other benefit coverage available to all employees, including seagoing, would be impossible to bear.

This was a crucial period for these independent unions. How could they answer the demands of their members who were being bombarded with literature from national unions extolling the virtues of their 20-year retirement package?—and it certainly had virtues, especially for those who did not look forward to going to sea for 40 years. And how could the marine management explain to others in their company that the 20-year retirement for seagoing personnel had become *prevailing,* and competitively must be met? Fortunately, marine managements had some ammunition. Employers bargaining with national unions had to increase sharply their contribution per-man, per-day in order to pay these 20-year pensions. This affected their competitive position. Also the question of adequate funding of the 20-year pensions negotiated by the national unions was a long way from being resolved. A further argument in the arsenal which marine managements used to convince "their people" (top management) to meet the demands of the independent unions in this area was that competing employers bargaining with national unions were required to contribute substantial amounts, per-day per-man, to pension-welfare plans. Furthermore *these plans were not geared directly to their employees, and were largely union-controlled.*

The arrangement whereby the employer contributes in excess of $25 per-day, per-man to a fund essentially controlled by the national union with which he bargains, has given that union additional power over that employee. Failure on the member's part to follow to the letter national-union rules and edicts could imperil his pension. This union-controlled pension plus the previously negotiated requirement that the employer must secure his officers from the union hiring hall, which operates on a *rotational* basis, made that control absolute. An officer who ships on vessels under contract to a national union is for better or for worse their man. The employer pays all and can say nothing.

This management of their employees by any union was something major oil companies wanted to avoid at all costs; nor did the vast majority of the officers employed by major oil companies in which independent unions were the bargaining representatives want to exchange the protection they had under the wide-ranging company benefit plans for the politically oriented benefit plans of the national unions. There were other drawbacks to representation by national unions. The history of the latter as far as work stoppages were concerned hardly could compare with the "never off pay" history which was one of the boasts of the independent union. But the 20-year pension issue presented problems.

The wheels of bargaining, like the wheels of justice, seem at times to grind slowly. Progress toward a 20-year pension proved this. And yet through patience and by persistence a method of meeting the 20-year retirement demand was worked out. It took different forms in different companies and was not secured in most instances in one step. The story of pension negotiations in several companies provides proof of how really different the personalities of companies are—even while attempting to resolve a similar issue. In this instance the question to be resolved was how to meet the demand of their officers for a 20-year pension that would be competitive with the ones already negotiated in the maritime industry by the various national unions representing deck officers, engineering officers, and radio officers (each group was represented by a different national union).

One company, American Trading and Production Corporation (not a petroleum company), which bargained with an independent union representing its deck and engineering officers, made a sincere and early (1966) effort to solve the pension problem by negotiating a "numbers" formula.[3] This was a combination of age and service—the magic number was 70—that would fulfill the requirement for a lifetime pension of $325 per month. For example, an officer age 43 with 27 years of service (totaling 70) would qualify. The numbers could be more or less in either of the categories. It was the combination that counted. This plan proved satisfactory for the time. A few years later a 20-year pension was negotiated in American Trading and Production almost identical with those in effect elsewhere in the maritime industry.

The first 20-year pension negotiated for seagoing officers by an independent union was bargained by the Mobil Tanker Officers Association. In 1965 the association had on its agenda a proposal for a supplementary pension plan.[4] This was not the first time the association had discussed an improved pension for seagoing officers. But inasmuch as industry had made specific moves in this direction, the association felt its arguments for a special seagoing retirement plan in Mobil now were strengthened.

However, the company was not ready to be the first major oil company to pioneer in pension improvements. They insisted that the association's proposal for a $325 a month pension after 20 years' sea service was "economically unsound," and that *in any event* the company was not prepared to participate in two pensions —their own and the special seagoing pension. They concluded their arguments at the time by stating again that the company pension plan was based on encouraging a man to make his career in Mobil—not to retire early and possibly work elsewhere.

Mobil, like other major oil companies, had a complete set of benefit plans that encompassed almost every area of protection needed by the average employee—life insurance, hospital and medical coverage, sick-leave with pay, a savings plan, and a better-than-average career pension plan. However, as with the other major oil companies, and practically all shore-based companies, pensions were predicated on a combination of earnings and years of service and the necessary age to secure the maximum benefit was 65—the presumed normal retirement age.

In the 1950s the MTOA proposed a plan whereby an officer could "phase out" his retirement. Starting at age 52—and working one month less each year (his normal work year was 8 months) he could, by age 60, be completely retired. The argument for this plan was that the company could continue to have his services, though for a lesser period each year, and new officers slowly could be funneled in at the lower ranks, thus making the transition smooth and painless to both the retiring officer and the company. But the proverbial stone wall was met when this and similar proposals for early retirement were made. Pension plans were the company's baby and they were not about to let someone else rock the cradle.

Knowing the attachment to, and pride in, their benefit plans that major oil companies had (and still have), it was not easy for the association to convince Mobil to grant a small segment of its employees a pension plan that would permit an officer to retire after 20 years of service regardless of age and receive $325 per month for the rest of his life. One can well imagine the raised eyebrows in the corporate boardroom when the directors first were told of this pension proposal. Even the chairman of the board could not, under the regular company plan, retire earlier than at age 55.

Furthermore, Mobil and the other major oil companies were troubled about "funding" the 20-year retirement plan. These companies were not "fly by night" shipping companies which could bail out of their responsibilities to their employees by declaring bankruptcy today to begin business tomorrow under a new name. They were substantial citizens of the community and their reputation for fair dealing with their employees meant a great deal to them. The problem therefore of financing such a potentially long-term obligation added to their distaste for it. The company continued to insist that the 20-year pension was wrong philosophically and that such a scheme could deprive the company (through early retirement) of experienced officers at an age when they were most valuable to them. Historically, the services of licensed officers between age 45 and 65 proved not only highly efficient, but in the area of judgment (so important for watch-standing officers whose decisions at sea could mean not only money but lives) their maturity generally guaranteed prudence. These attributes the company was loath to lose.

Negotiations with all major oil companies for 20-year pensions were traumatic. Company representatives literally ranted and raved about the idiocy of so early a retirement with so little service. But the various bargaining committees had two strong arguments going for them. First, a 20-year pension had become industry practice, and industry was paying for this through sharply increased contributions to the national-union welfare and pension plans. Second, seagoing personnel were different, *very different,* from shore-based employees. They were "captives" aboard ship for 24 hours every day a ship was at sea, and many times in port as well—especially if the port was not the individual's home port. Despite the fact that vacations had increased substantially there remained the very real disadvantage of being away from home for long periods of time, and over a long span of years. Shorten the span at least, argued the various independent tanker associations. Finally this was done. Mobil was the first of the major oil companies to negotiate a 20-year retirement for its seagoing officers, and it exacted a price for it. The price was a substitution of a new set of benefit plans for the existing more attractive ones.[5]

On February 24, 1967, the executive committee of the MTOA wrote to the membership regarding the results of meetings with the company on an improved pension plan. Indicating the long history of the efforts made to improve the company plan for seagoing officers, the association at the outset stated:

> As you know, your present Executive Committee, as have past Executive Committees, have been endeavoring to secure an improved pension plan. We have been trying to do this without disturbing any of the existing Mobil Benefit Plans. We have also been trying to do this without sacrificing any base wages. (In 1966 a wage increase in the industry averaging sixty dollars a month was directed by the national unions toward the twenty-year pension, to help finance it.) [6]

In their report the executive committee stated that on February 16 the company gave the association proposals aimed at meeting the association's demand for improved pensions for seagoing officers. The committee pointed out that:

> ... the new Plan proposed by the Company would provide substantial improved benefits, particularly for an officer between the ages of 55 and 60, compared with what he would receive under the present plan. However, you will also note that to achieve this an officer would have to terminate his participation in the present Company Annuity and Insurance Plan, which also would include the Savings Plan and all Plans. To replace the other plans you will note the Company proposed new benefit plans which however would not provide the same benefits as are provided under the existing Company benefit plans.[7]

At the time the committee informed the company that they would study the company's proposals and return after a few days to discuss the proposals further. They did this on February 22 and at that time, in addition to discussing the company's proposals and asking specific questions regarding them, the association made certain counter-proposals. The thrust of these meetings was the company's intention, or hope, to meet the association's demands by providing the association with a brand-new set of benefits which would be substituted for the company-wide benefit plans.

In other words, the price that would have to be paid for an improved seagoing pension plan, one that would not even include a 20-year sea-service regardless-of-age pension, was a scuttling of the regular benefit plans under which all employees at the time were covered.

By proposing a new set of "benefits" as a substitute for those provided by the overall company benefit package, the company pointed out that these "benefits" could be modified by bargaining. In effect, bargaining by the MTOA could be done with regard to a special Marine Benefits Program. Bargaining company-wide benefits by the MTOA alone could not be done since the MTOA represented fewer than 150 employees compared with the several thousand employed nation-wide by Mobil. Their company-wide pension plan, Mobil maintained, was inviolate. It could not be fragmented to satisfy the aspirations of each bargaining unit which from its viewpoint could justify the particular changes it desired. Countless days were spent trying to design a formula that would meet the demands of the MTOA and that would not fracture the company's benefit-plan structure. But to no avail. The company's insistence that if the "seagoing" wanted the industry 20-year pension they would have to give up the regular company benefit plans, the association considered a callous position.

At this time the association's executive committee was willing to make some compromises especially in the age factor if they could at least retain participation in the company savings plan (which had been a real money-maker for everyone who participated in it) and if the pension benefits could be increased beyond 20 years of service to age 55. Nothing, however, was accomplished at these meetings except an exchange of ideas between the association and the company and a thorough examination of the company's proposals with respect to both its pluses and its minuses.

The company's proposals (unacceptable as they were to the association's negotiating committee) nevertheless were sent to the fleet for review and comment. The reply received from one of the vessels was typical of the angry reaction of the fleet. On April 18, 1967, a meeting of the officers aboard the s.s. *Colina* was held. A six-page letter embodying the minutes of the meeting was sent to the association. It was reproduced as received and sent to the other vessels. Excerpts from these minutes clearly convey the negative reaction to the company proposal on pension improvement.

> Old Business: The BIG LIE commonly referred to as The Marine Benefit Program is a dead issue with all Officers on this ship. We simply dismissed this program as a sham, a game played by Gulf–East Coast Management for its own amusement and in its own interest. The Company just used it as a gimmick to stall for time, to delay and dodge the issue, and to see what the outcome would be between the S.V.T.M.A. and O.C.A.W. [the independent union representing the unlicensed seamen in Mobil were about to affiliate with the AFL–CIO Oil and Chemical Workers]. The integrity of the Management of the Gulf–East Coast Operations, in the eyes of the Fleet Officers has suffered a severe setback. Thousands of Officers in the Maritime Industry are already covered by an early retirement plan—why not Mobil?
> Our instructions to the Executive Committee is to forget the "BIG LIE" and concentrate and direct all its efforts and resources to secure, for all Fleet Officers, an early retirement plan based on 20 years' service, regardless of age, with a minimum level of benefits starting at $400 per month, escalating to a maximum level of benefits at 30 years of service of 62.4% of basic wages. The "BIG LIE" is nothing but a red herring.[8]

The concluding paragraphs of these minutes castigate the company for what the officers considered to be its planned inaction. At the same time, the members on the s.s. *Colina* renewed their support of the association and its executive committee. The pension battle was crucial; though finally won, it produced some casualties.

> All Fleet Officers are encouraged to join the fight for early retirement pensions and improved working agreement. Today, when everything moves at such a fast rate, the pleasure of becoming deeply involved in S.V.T.O.A. [the independent union] affairs can easily be lost. Without such involvement, some Officers become complacent—eternally subjected to the conflicting tides of circumstance and other peoples' opinions.
> What passes for Labor–Management relations in Gulf–East Coast Operations has taken so many weird twists in the past few weeks that the net effect on Fleet Officers comes close to being unbelievable.
> The Company's urge for inaction at this time is, of course, understandable if not commendable. The Company can afford such inaction but not Fleet Officers, if they are to realize their dream of early retirement with 20 years of service regardless of age. All Fleet Officers are urged to pay their dues and give their *full support* to the newly elected Executive Committee.[9]

The airing of the company's pension proposal to the fleet did some good. It reinforced the executive committee in its opposition to certain parts of the company's earlier benefit plan proposal. On August 7, 1967, the association gave the company a set of proposals for a new agreement. The committee made these introductory remarks:

> As this Committee understands it, our purpose in meeting with the Company is to continue our discussions with the Company on an improved pension and retirement plan. As you well know, the Company proposal to change the existing pension plan, made to the Association some months ago, was entirely unsatisfactory and was rejected by the Executive Committee.
>
> (1) RETIREMENT & PENSION: Therefore, in accordance with our letter to the Company dated June 29, 1967, we expect that the Company is prepared to present to the Association an improved pension and early retirement plan. We believe that it is important for you to know that such an improvement in early retirement and pensions must provide that any officer may at his option retire from the Company at any age provided he has twenty years service. This is the practice in the bulk of the industry today and we certainly feel that the officers in Mobil are entitled to at least the same consideration.[10]

The company had improved substantially its offer made in February, but when they began to bargain in August, a part of their proposal required that the officer who had 20 years of sea service *also be 50 years of age,* or over, in order to retire and receive the new pension. This was a serious stumbling-block. It is pertinent to point out that two of the four members of the then-executive committee of the association were anxious to retire under a 20-year plan, but neither of them had reached age 50. It is difficult to say how much their personal desires to retire under a 20-year, no-age plan contributed to the company's final agreement to remove the age factor and have the plan based on 20 years' service regardless of age,* but their desire did add a strong personal concern which strengthened the association's arguments and acted as a barrier to any agreement that would have required a specific retirement age. In the association's story to the membership they stated:

> Your Association's Executive Committee insisted that good as this plan might be (it was quite an improvement over the plan

---

* Both of these members did retire as soon as the new pension plan was ratified by the membership.

submitted by the Company in February) it would not be acceptable to the Executive Committee unless it was based on twenty years of sea service at *any age*. This insistence by the Executive Committee on the elimination of age 50 resulted in the Company changing its proposal to be what it now is, namely, twenty years–any age.[11]

On September 26, 1967, in a Special Bulletin to the membership, the executive committee announced that at long last they had surmounted the hurdle on pensions; they had secured a 20-year retirement agreement, without regard to age. The executive committee was both happy and sad with the results of their efforts—happy because they had pierced the wall of opposition to a separate pension plan for seagoing officers that the company had erected over many years, but sad because to accomplish this they had had to settle for a new set of marine benefits which provided less in the areas of sick-leave pay and insurance; and there would be no savings plan.

There were other economic gains made at these negotiations and in general the executive committee was pleased with the overall results of the negotiations. On the pension question, the executive committee informed the membership:

> As we all know the question of early retirement has been on the minds and lips of every officer in this fleet for at least six years. Past Committees tried and tried hard to break through the Company's overall pension plan to provide earlier retirement for seagoing officers. Now, as you will note from reading the Agreement which we have signed and which is submitted to you for your approval or disapproval, any officer with twenty years credited service will be able to retire regardless of his age. We mention this as item number one before we get to the story of our negotiations because we know that this is what every officer is anxious to hear.[12]

The benefits provided under the now-negotiated early-retirement plan according to the story given to the fleet were as follows:

> An officer who retires will receive a monthly pension for life equal to a percentage of his final average pay. This includes continuous-service pay.* After 20 years he will receive 32.5% of average pay. This continues at the rate of 2% per year for the next five years until it reaches 42.5% of final average pay after 25 years of service. After this it will increase further but not at

---

* Additional compensation based on length of service as an officer.

the same rate. For each additional year it will increase ¼% per year. So that, for example, a man with 40 years of service would receive 46.25% of his final average pay. Since this pay is currently higher as starting pay than national-union agreements provide and since in addition there is added to this his continuous-service pay, this percentage of his final pay will give him more dollars than national union plans provide.

Furthermore, there will be a minimum of $325 per month for a licensed officer who completes twenty years of service (this is identical with national unions). This minimum will be increased by $20 per month for each additional year up to twenty-five years. So that an officer with twenty-five years of service regardless of age may retire under this plan and receive a minimum of $425 per month. Social Security benefits are in addition to this retirement pay.[13]

It was clear that the older officers who had in excess of 20 years of service and who were age 50 and beyond would fare better under the overall company benefit plans including retirement. Therefore, in fairness to these officers the company agreed with the association to give all the officers the option of accepting the new marine benefits program or remaining in the existing plans. Once the choice was made it could not be changed. New officers would be covered by the new marine benefits program. Some idea of the vast difference in the amount of pension payable under the existing company pension compared with the proposed plan may be noted from the following figures:

TABLE VIII
TYPICAL PENSIONS UNDER THE PROPOSED FORMULA OF 37½% PLUS ½% AFTER AGE 55 PLUS 20 YEARS OF SERVICE LESS ½ OF THE PRIMARY SOCIAL SECURITY BENEFIT PAYABLE AT AGE 62[14]

	Age 55, 20 yrs. serv.		Age 60, 25 yrs. serv.		Age 65, 30 yrs. serv.	
	Present	Proposed	Present	Proposed	Present	Proposed
Master	$206.08	$587.25	$373.08	$614.40	$682.50	$651.55
Chief Engineer	197.08	566.62	356.67	591.40	652.50	628.17
CM–1AE	133.58	388.12	241.83	402.00	442.50	425.87
2M–2AE	111.00	330.00	200.91	340.00	367.50	360.00
3M–3AE	97.41	289.87	176.33	297.00	322.50	314.52

For example, a second mate or second assistant engineer at that time aged 55 with 20 years of service would under the existing company plan have a retirement of only $111 per month; whereas under the proposed plan he would receive $330 per month. On the other hand, a master retiring at the normal retirement age of 65 with 30 years of service would fare better under the existing company plan than he would under the proposed 20-year retirement plan. Under the regular company plan he would receive $682.50 per month; under the proposed early-retirement plan he would receive $651.55 per month. Obviously, the plan was for the younger officers with service in the neighborhood of 20 years. Furthermore, the older officers by remaining in the company retirement plan also would continue to participate in the other company benefits including the savings plan. These as a package were distinctly superior to the new marine benefits program. The result was that the majority of the senior officers chose to remain in the existing company benefit plans.

Despite its drawbacks the newly negotiated pension in Mobil, together with wage and other changes, when submitted to the membership was overwhelmingly approved. The vote was 60 to 39.[15] Soon however another problem arose. Restrictions on future seagoing employment for those who retired under the 20-year, any-age plan were severe. Under this "restricted employment" clause contained in the Memorandum of Understanding dated September 23, 1967 was this statement: "In consideration of the pension payments provided under the program retired employees shall agree not to engage in seafaring employment." [16] * When the full import of this restriction was realized, the association sought to have it softened. There was an honest difference of opinion between the parties as to what was intended in the case of an officer who retired under the 20-year plan. Would he lose his pension forever should he return to seafaring employment, or only have his pension payments suspended during such periods of resumed seagoing employment?

There were seemingly fruitless discussions on the question of loss of pension where an officer returned to seafaring employment after accepting the 20-year retirement. The company argued that for years they had listened to the association's plea that seagoing personnel be permitted to retire to be ashore with their families *before* the twilight of their lives—a period longer than the regular company pension provided. Returning to sea, the company

---

* Restriction on seagoing employment exists in the 20-year, any-age retirement plans negotiated by national unions.

pointed out, would defeat this objective. The company was adamant in their refusal to make any exceptions.

On June 7 the association proposed taking the matter of interpreting the restricted-employment clause to arbitration, but no agreement could be reached on the definition of the question to be arbitrated.[17] After further discussions the company agreed to modify this provision. They did this by a letter to the association on August 14, 1968:

> The basis for the Marine Benefits Program for Licensed Officers is the memorandum of understanding between ourselves dated September 23, 1967. As you know, this document contains the following clause:
>
> RESTRICTED EMPLOYMENT
> In consideration of the pension payments provided under the program retired employees shall agree not to engage in seafaring employment.
>
> In negotiating this language, it was our clear intention that employees retiring under this plan would forgo all future seafaring employment. Accordingly, we have established an administrative rule whereby the pension of an employee retired under this plan will be terminated if he engages in seafaring employment, unless such service is with Mobil.
>
> You have brought to our attention the possibility that unforeseen circumstances may arise under which an employee retired under this plan might find it necessary to return to sea at a time when employment with Mobil may not be available. In recognition of this fact, and without prejudice to our position as stated above, we are prepared to grant such retired employees permission to return to sea for limited periods, as follows.[18]

The permission which the company granted would allow a retired officer to return to seafaring employment for a maximum period of 24 months. When such employment terminated he was to surrender his Merchant Mariner's Document to the Coast Guard. Then his pension would be resumed. The final paragraph of the company's letter states:

> Permission to return to seafaring employment will be conditional upon the retired employee's acceptance of the foregoing terms. The pensions of retired employees who return to seafaring employment without obtaining prior company permission will be terminated. Please return one copy of this letter signed, to indicate your understanding and acceptance of the foregoing.[19]

This was acceptable to the executive committee, at least until the matter could be reviewed further during negotiations for the next agreement. These took place in December of 1968. At this time the company softened still further their stand on retired (i.e., retired under the special early retirement plan) officers' returning to sea. In a letter dated December 12, 1968, and agreed to by the association's executive committee, the company stated:

> The purpose of this letter is to set forth the administrative procedure by which the Company will certify continuing eligibility for pension payments applied for under the Marine Benefits Program for Licensed Officers dated September 23, 1967. This letter supersedes our letter of August 14, 1968.
> 1. Seafaring employment shall mean employment as a Master or a Licensed or unlicensed member of the crew aboard any self-propelled U. S. flag vessel whose U.S.C.G. Certificate of Inspection permits "ocean" operation.
> 2. In the event an employee retires and subsequently returns to seafaring employment, pension payments shall be suspended for any calendar month in which he is so employed or is receiving pay for vacation earned by such employment during all or part of the month.
> 3. Retired employees who engage in seafaring employment must notify the company promptly in writing of the details of such employment. Retired employees who engage in seafaring employment and fail to notify the company shall return all pension payments which would otherwise have been suspended. Failure to return such pension payments will be cause for cancellation of any future pension payments.
> 4. In the case of a retired employee who returns to seafaring employment and thereby has pension payments suspended, the company will continue to reduce the retired death benefit as if the suspended payment had actually been paid.
>
> Very truly yours,
> C. S. TOWNSHEND, *Manager*
> Gulf–East Coast Operations[20]

These negotiations and letters of interpretation did not end the pension question forever, but they did clarify the situation and established a special seagoing retirement plan competitive with that negotiated by national unions representing seagoing personnel. But though the new plan was a slight improvement over national-union plans as far as actual dollars of retirement income was concerned, the severing of Mobil seagoing officers from the regular company benefit plans, especially the savings plan, was a heavy price to pay. In the opinion of the association this stand hardly could help the company's image, since encouraging orientation toward the company as a beneficent employer was a basic reason for the establishment of the plans in the first place.

When other major oil companies bargaining with their licensed officers via independent unions subsequently negotiated 20-year retirement plans *without* requiring their officers to sacrifice participation in the regular company benefit plans, the inequity of the Mobil situation became more acute. But a bargain is a bargain, and at the time the 20-year plan was negotiated in Mobil no major oil company had moved that far. This at least was a move in the right direction, and it did break the log-jam of opposition to the 20-year retirement concept that major oil companies had maintained so tenaciously for so long.

NOTES

1. Agreement, January 14, 1946, JSTOA–Standard Oil Company (N.J.), Marine Department.
2. Masters, Mates and Pilots (Atlantic and Gulf Districts), *Pension*, New York, no imprint. Marine Engineers' Beneficial Association, *MEBA Pension Trust Regulations,* effective January 1, 1956, New York, no imprint.
3. Agreement, November 1, 1966, ATOA and American Trading and Production Corp.
4. Negotiations, MTOA, Mobil Oil Company, 1965, MTOA Official Records, New York.
5. Memorandum of Understanding, MTOA and Mobil Oil Company, September 23, 1967.
6. Letter (mimeographed), to all members from Executive Committee, MTOA, February 24, 1967.
7. *Ibid.*
8. Letter, from MTOA members aboard s.s. *Colina,* April 18, 1967.
9. *Ibid.*
10. MTOA Proposals to Mobil Oil Company, August 7, 1967.
11. Letter, MTOA Executive Committee to membership, September 10, 1967.
12. Special Bulletin, from MTOA Executive Committee to membership, September 26, 1967.
13. *Ibid.*
14. Table, comparison of pensions under the proposed new benefits formula with existing Mobil benefit plans.
15. Ratification Ballot, MTOA, November 1, 1967.
16. Memorandum of Understanding, MTOA and Mobil Oil Company, September 23, 1967.
17. Letter, MTOA to Mobil Oil Company, June 7, 1968.
18. Letter, Mobil Oil Company to MTOA, August 14, 1968.
19. *Ibid.*
20. Letter, Mobil Oil Company to MTOA, December 12, 1968.

3

More on Pension Bargaining—Texaco Does It Differently

TEXACO FACED THE EARLY-PENSION PROPOSAL differently and resolved it in stages. The company had both an attractive pension plan predicated on an employee's remaining until the normal retirement age of 65 or receiving a somewhat reduced retirement income if he retired between the ages of 55 and 65. Also, the company had established a savings plan which encouraged employees to put substantial sums aside, since the company matched the employee's 6% participation by 3% for a total of 9%. These monies could be invested in a variety of ways at the discretion of the employees.

The other fringe benefits in Texaco (which included full pay when sick and substantial life insurance) compared more than favorably with benefits national unions had been able to provide by their requirement that companies contribute so many dollars per-day per-man to fund a pension and welfare plan. Nevertheless, Texaco officers, deck, engine, and radio, argued strongly for a seagoing pension after 20 years of sea service, regardless of age. This had become a fact of life in the national unions for seagoing officers and some similar arrangement had to be provided through bargaining between Texaco and the TTOA. Although the argument from comparison generally is convincing, in the instance of the 20-year pensions each company in its own fashion opposed it. Some companies offered—at least in the early stages of negotiations—a modification of their company-wide pension plan that covered all employees. As early as 1965 Texaco in negotiations with the TTOA had offered to modify the existing company pension plan by *guaranteeing* an officer with 20 years in Texaco, *and age 55,* the right to retire with $325 a month. Commenting on what was bargained at the time the association in its report to its members stated:

True, this doesn't affect many Texaco officers, who if they are now young will have built up substantially more than $325 when they are age 55. Nor does it benefit the senior officer who is over 55 and who already has built up considerably more than the $325 per month.

One thing we believe should be borne in mind regarding pensions (and this is basic and terribly important to the individual officer and to his *family*) and that is the fact that the Texaco pension plan is guaranteed. It is fully funded. There need be no fear as to whether or not the money will be there when the officer retires. Secondly, the pension under the Texaco plan is based on a man's years of service and earnings so that every time we improve the wages we automatically improve our pensions.

This is not to indicate that there will be any slowing down in our efforts to secure a special pension for seagoing officers but it is meant to emphasize the protection which the Texaco officers now have as far as pensions are concerned.[1]

The company's move was minimal, but at least it was in the right direction. In retrospect one realizes the monumental job of a marine management endeavoring to meet the desires of their licensed officers in the light of competitive conditions in the maritime industry. It was difficult to convince the fringe-benefit staff that competition from national unions in this area made matching a "must." Understandably, they were worried about carving up the company "benefits package," which they had so painstakingly put together for *all* Texaco employees. The association made mention at the time that, according to a published report, one of the national-union pension plans for seagoing officers had a liability of $100,000,000 and that, since the plan was not funded (it was on a "pay as you go" basis), there were not the guarantees which were true of pensions in Texaco. In their concluding remarks to the membership the association stated:

What can happen to such a pension plan and those who are putting their hopes in it, down the road, we don't know, but frankly we like our Texaco pension plan with the guarantees it has and we will continue to pursue improvements in pensions *also on a guaranteed basis.*[2]

Texaco's situation was somewhat different compared to that in Esso or Getty. On the same ship there were three unions—the unlicensed seamen were represented by the National Maritime Union (AFL–CIO); the deck officers and engineers were represented by the Texaco Tanker Officers Associations (Ind.); and the radio officers were represented by the Texaco Radio Officers Association (Ind.). With respect to the first group, the company in dealing with the National Maritime Union paid so many dollars per-day per-man (the figure constantly increased) to the union's pension and welfare plan. From this fund the union provided pensions, hospitalization, and other benefits of a similar nature—not to Texaco employees as such, but to members of the National Maritime Union who qualified.

Since the National Maritime Union was the recognized union for unlicensed personnel aboard Texaco ships, seamen employed on their vessels, under the rules of the union pension and welfare plan, would qualify for various payments. However, the company did not make these payments directly to the Texaco employees who sailed on their vessels as members of the unlicensed personnel. These seamen (although the monies paid by Texaco made possible their vacation pay, pensions, and welfare) actually were employees of the National Maritime Union which physically provided these benefits and effectively controlled the conditions under which the seamen became eligible.

The situation with respect to the deck and engine officers, as well as the radio officers, was different. These officers were full-time employees of Texaco and were treated, generally speaking, the same as the company's shoreside employees. Their vacations and various other fringe benefits were in accordance with company plans and/or agreements negotiated with the two independent unions, the TTOA and the TROA.

Texaco was well aware of the need to meet certain changes that had occurred in the maritime industry, especially in the area of pensions. They already had moved somewhat in this direction but not to the extent that prevailed under agreements made by national unions representing deck officers, engineering officers, and radio officers. However, while they may have moved slowly, they moved with a serious concern for their pledged word to their employees, as well as with due regard to the interests of their stockholders and, of course, constantly cognizant of the need to remain competitive. In a special bulletin sent to the membership of the TTOA on October 10, 1967, following the completion of negotiations for a new agreement, the headline read as follows:

> TTOA executive committee successfully negotiates 7% increase in base wage: 8% increase in overtime and tank cleaning: improvement in transportation: pay for the five days which masters and chief engineers work but have not been receiving compensa-

tion because of being paid on a monthly basis: agreement by the company to meet with the association on all items in the agreement by February 1, 1968: *and negotiate at that time a competitive pension plan*: Also pilot program to start for port relief north of Hatteras. Wages and overtime effective September 1, 1967 provided agreement is ratified by membership.[3]

Probably the most important part of this announcement was the fact that early in 1968 the company indicated they would be ready to negotiate a competitive pension plan. The company and the association began their negotiations to accomplish this in February of 1968. Various concepts were studied how best to arrive at the kind of pension which would be competitive, which would meet the desires of the Texaco officers, one for which Texaco could afford the cost, and above all *which would be guaranteed*.

In an interim report made on the 15th of February the association reviewed the status of negotiations with the company and summarized four different concepts that were under consideration in the current negotiations. Depending upon the formula used in each of these concepts the amounts of pension varied, especially where years of service were meaningful. Some idea of what both sides were talking about may be gained from the association's presentation to the membership of "the fourth concept":

(4) The Fourth Concept, and one on which more time was spent than any of the others, was to take the highest five-year wage received in the last ten years of service, including an average length of service increase, for a particular rating.

Using this "high five" base pay, plus an average length of service increase and using as an example an officer with 20 years of service, here is how the present figures would compare in dollars with what the national unions will be able to receive after their new plan goes into effect on June 16, 1968. This fourth concept is based on 33% of Texaco wages, including an average length of service increase for a 20-year officer. Under this a Texaco master could receive $589 compared with a master under the national union agreement of $521.

Chief mate–first assistant in Texaco could receive $397. Chief mate–first assistant under national unions could receive $370.[4]

Because of the tremendous financial commitments involved in the establishment of a funded and guaranteed early-pension such as Texaco officers desired, a further recess was necessary until May 21, 1968 to enable the company to assess the cost, based on certain assumptions especially as to the number of officers with

20 years of service who would elect to retire under the proposed plan. For example, the cost would be far greater in the case of an officer, aged 41, who chose to retire and receive for the rest of his life a minimum pension of $325 per month, compared with the officer who remained until age 55 or 60.

From May 21 to May 27 the bargaining that took place examined every aspect of the 20-year pension, since this had become the paramount issue in the fleet and the members were anxiously awaiting the outcome. Finally, the association and the company reached agreement. This was a real victory for the association. Their patience and determination had won for their members a 20-year pension superior to that negotiated by national unions in the maritime industry—*and without sacrificing any of the company benefit plans* as had been done in Mobil.

It is not to be expected that individuals who did not participate in bargaining on a subject as involved as the establishment of a pension of this type should immediately grasp the various refinements that became a part of the final agreement; nor are these details completely essential to convey how substantial the pension improvement was to the fleet officers. However, there were two interesting areas in the Texaco plan which do deserve comment. As a *quid pro quo* for the 20-year pension plan the company in its original proposal asked the association to give the company the unqualified right to retire an officer after 20 years. This the association refused, since so worded, the 20-year pension plan could become—if the company so chose—an automatic discharge without cause. The second aspect in these negotiations for a 20-year pension plan was the desire of the association to continue the "savings plan" inviolate. Here again they were successful. This is best explained in the excerpt from the negotiations story of May 28, 1968:

> When the company first made their proposal they insisted (as you will note in the enclosure which we are sending to you with this story) that they take credit after June 1, 1968 for the pension equivalent of the company's contribution to the employee savings plan. This is what has been done both in Humble [Exxon] and Tidewater [Getty] in their pension agreements. We do not want to be immodest about our success in getting this provision *out* of the company proposal, but we must tell you that we argued strenuously that the confusion that would result for all of us in trying to determine the so-called equivalent pension value of the company's contribution to the savings plan would be so

great as to lessen the true value of this pension. Furthermore, we strongly felt that the employee savings plan should not be touched *at all*.[5]

A further feature of these negotiations and one related directly to the 20-year pension was a surprise offer by the company of a confidential deferred-compensation plan. By its terms Texaco would compensate their officers with a substantial sum annually (in the case of masters and chief engineers the amount was $1,500), up to half of which would be paid currently. The remainder would be put into an account for each officer and would not be available until he attained age 55. The purpose of this was to offset the obvious attractiveness for the younger officer of being able to retire after 20 years with a strong financial incentive to remain with Texaco at least until age 55. Based on the fact that few officers have availed themselves of the opportunity to retire early, the purpose of the deferred compensation plan appears to have been achieved.

The substantial approval vote (117 to 50) by the membership was sufficient reward for the efforts of the elected and unpaid members of the executive committee. It represented a collective "well done." In a larger sense it was eloquent testimony to the bargaining ability of the members of the committee as well as the demonstration of the desire of Texaco to meet the legitimate demands of their officers both realistically and generously. Texaco officers in turn were proud of their association and had further proof that they were accepted as an integral part of the Texaco family.

NOTES

1. TTOA, *News Letter,* May 1, 1965.
2. *Ibid.*
3. TTOA, *Bulletin,* October 10, 1967.
4. TTOA, *News Letter,* February 15, 1968.
5. TTOA, *News Letter,* May 28, 1968.

4

The Humble Way

HUMBLE (NOW EXXON) AND THE ASSOCIATION representing its licensed officers—the Jersey Standard Tanker Officers Association (JSTOA)—met the problem of pensions in still another way. The subject of improved pensions, which had been on the agenda of the association for years during the various bargaining sessions with the company, had become more pressing in the fall of 1965. At this time, the association's executive committee had invited representatives from major insurance companies to analyze the pension problem and determine how much additional money was necessary to enable an officer to retire sooner than the company pension plan permitted and receive a satisfactory annuity.

National unions had sacrificed at least one 6 per cent wage increase to help provide the funds for their improved pensions. Why not try that approach? Anticipating how many officers would retire at what age was, for the the insurance companies, no better than an educated guess. As a result, the figures supplied by the insurance companies, based on a translation of a 6 per cent wage increase into pensions, fell far short of the goal desired by the association, and so it was thought better to bargain directly with the company for the best early-retirement plan possible.

Prior to actual negotiations, in the fall of 1965, the association, reporting the results of the election for two executive committee members, strongly criticized those who by not voting were demonstrating an apathy toward the association that could endanger its future. The executive committee comprised four seagoing officers —two from the deck department and two from the engine department. They held office for two years. Each year two were elected to avoid the possibility of a completely new committee every two years.

The *JSTOA News Letter* of August 11, 1965 emphasized the difficulties of a democratically run organization in which membership was voluntary. Officers were not required to join the JSTOA in order to be employed or remain employed. National unions did not have this problem. By their rules, shipping is done from a union hiring hall. Obedience to the union's established rules included the payment of initiation fee and dues—both of which were substantial. The power to coerce is always inviting, whether practiced by a company, a union, or the government. While the *News Letter* of August 11 does not detail all the internal problems of an independent union, at least it throws some light on some of the problems in this one. Here are selections from it:

APATHY—THE ENEMY OF PROGRESS AND THE OPEN DOOR TO DISINTEGRATION.

The vote in the above election for members of the Executive Committee, frankly, is appalling. If the interest shown in the JSTOA is measured by the number of members who have voted in this last election, this can become a very serious matter. Let's put our cards on the table. The JSTOA for more than 27 years has functioned in behalf of *all* the officers in the Esso fleet. It has operated under all kinds of circumstances—large fleets, declining fleets, fleets at war, and fleets at peace. It has negotiated sharp wage-increases on countless occasions. It has pioneered in paid leave plans that became the talk of the industry (and which national unions only of recent date have begun to follow).

It has participated through negotiations in Early Retirement Plans. It negotiated the first War Bonus in World War II. These are just a few of the considerable things done for *all* the officers by the JSTOA. And, frankly, these were done in large measure because of the interest shown by the average officer.

Today there is a certain small group of officers who smugly take what the JSTOA has negotiated for them but never as much as lift a finger—either a financial finger or any other kind of finger—to give positive assistance to the JSTOA in its various efforts. Most of these groups are the moaners and groaners for whom if you stood on your head you couldn't satisfy them. And in many instances, these very people can be found giving aid and comfort to national unions. The fact is that if a national union came into the Esso Fleet they along with everyone else would pay and pay and pay (unless, of course, some of them are already on the payroll of a national union and thereby conveniently are working both sides of the street). . . .

And now to the members who are good supporting members, financially speaking, but who take the attitude that it isn't necessary to vote, that think things will be all right anyway. Things are never all right in this world and they never will be all right as long as there are people. The best that can be done to make the world nearly all right is to have intelligent, decent people showing sufficient interest—where they have the opportunity to have their own organization—in that organization and in its activities.[1]

This appeal for support from non-members and for more participation from members brought results. This and similar efforts were perennially necessary to maintain both the membership itself and to stimulate activity.

The 1965 negotiations were stymied by the apparent unwillingness of the company's bargaining team to promise progress on pension-plan changes. The executive committee, more in annoyance than in despair, sent a telegram to Joseph Andreae, Manager of Humble's Marine Department at Houston, Texas, to break the log-jam.[2] The telegram emphasized the long-standing desire of the fleet officers to be treated differently from shoreside employees in the matter of pensions for the reason that most of their working careers were spent away from home. It also stressed the known fact of the moves of national unions in this area.

Shortly thereafter, Andreae came to New York and met with the executive committee. He admitted that the special category of licensed seagoing officers required special treatment, particularly in the area of pensions. At that time, he authorized the company's bargaining committee to pursue a study with the association with a view toward reaching a mutually satisfactory solution on pensions. Meanwhile, bargaining on other matters, which had begun in late October 1965, continued. Agreement on an amendment to the existing contract finally was reached February 10, 1966. In the concluding paragraphs of the negotiation story to the fleet the executive committee stated:

> All the grievances that the Association had with the Company have been resolved with the exception of one. This has proceeded to Step #4 in the grievance procedure as outlined in the Agreement and we will report to the membership on its outcome.
>
> Again we wish to thank each and every member of the Association for his patience in awaiting the outcome of these long and difficult negotiations. We believe that the membership will agree that gains have been made in the areas most desired, namely, base wages retroactive to November 1, 1965; overtime rate retroactive to November 1, 1965; full-hour supper retroactive to November 1, 1965; overtime for correcting charts effective upon ratification; and improvements in working conditions in shipyard. These are meaningful items to every officer and benefits in every area, such as pensions and sick leave, will be affected in an upward manner by these money improvements. But most important of all

is the breakthrough in the *recognition by the Company that seagoing officers should receive special consideration as far as pensions are concerned because they do go to sea,* and the fact that the Company has agreed to a study is a milestone of no mean proportions.[3]

Progress on pensions was slow. Nevertheless on August 18, 1966, the JSTOA sensed something was developing and warned officers who were contemplating retirement to "wait and see."

The *JSTOA News Letter*s were found to be the best means of informing the officers of bargaining progress as well as communicating with the membership on other matters.

J.S.T.O.A.   NEWS LETTER   8/18/66

PENSION IMPROVEMENT COMING, WE BELIEVE.

Based on the efforts made by the Executive Committee of the JSTOA and their Adviser over the past two years, which included serious studies of the various pension plans and ways by which our pension for seagoing personnel could be improved, we believe that in the relatively near future we will be able to submit to the membership an improved pension plan.

While we are not certain about this, we feel that we should alert every officer who may have in mind now to retire early so that, if we are successful in obtaining an improved pension, this particular officer will not have already retired under the existing plan. Therefore, we trust that every officer who is thinking about retiring will hold off for at least 60 days. You are all familiar with the efforts made by the Association in the past to move this pension question off dead center. Based on our last negotiations we believe we have moved it off dead center. In fact, we are certain of this.

What the particular pension improvement will be after we meet with the Company, which will be shortly, we cannot tell you. But based upon our conversations with the Company and on studies they have been making, we feel quite sure that at least as far as seagoing personnel are concerned in the Humble fleet, there will be an improvement. The telegram below indicates how close we are to a meaningful meeting with the Company.

Telegram sent to Humble Oil & Refining Company on August 17, 1966:

At our last negotiations we were told orally and by telegram from Mr. Andreae that meetings to come up with a satisfactory pension plan that would recognize the special status of seagoing personnel would be accomplished with reasonable certainty prior to our next regular negotiations this fall. While we have had a couple meetings, nothing meaningful has been accomplished. We had expected to meet with the Company Representative early in the week of August 2. We still expect to meet sometime in the week of August 22 or at the very latest during the week of August 29. When we meet we trust based upon what the Company has indicated that a satisfactory plan will be available for our joint discussions.

Three members of the Executive Committee are presently on paid leave and will continue to be available in order that this matter so important to all the officers in the fleet may be resolved. May we have your firm commitment on the date of our next meeting.

JERSEY STANDARD TANKER OFFICERS ASSOCIATION[4]

There still was some delay, but both sides finally met early in the fall for the primary purpose of pension discussion and the resolution of this paramount issue. When the company presented its proposal for an improved pension and the executive committee examined it, they were happily surprised. The proposal was a generous one. The announcement of it and a description of how it worked appeared in a special JSTOA *Bulletin* dated November 15, 1966.[5]

The thrust of the improved pension plan was the opportunity offered seagoing officers to retire with a substantially improved pension at age 55 or beyond. It gave officers who had decided that age 55 was their target date to retire a far larger pension than was possible under the regular Humble Annuity Plan. And there were no strings attached. No benefit plans were eliminated or reduced to secure it. As the association's *Bulletin* described it,

> The plan is not compulsory. No officer must retire under it. An officer who retires under the plan may work anywhere that he wishes and continue to receive his full retirement income. He may work at sea or ashore or not at all. The decision is entirely up to him. His retirement income will not be affected by his decision. The supplement [the full name was Special Sea Service Retirement Annuity Supplement] will be paid as regular annuities are paid. It will be a lifetime annuity with a sixty-month certainty.[6]

Under the formula of this supplement a captain with 30 years' service, age 55, whose average wage for his last 5 years was $1,650 per month, could retire with a lifetime monthly income of $722. The special supplement part of this $722 was $277. In short, this was the *extra* retirement income that the association rightfully could claim to be the result of their efforts over several years. Insurance company figures indicate that to buy an individual age 55 one dollar per-month of annuity for life costs $195. Using these figures, the additional $277 per month for this officer could cost the company $54,015, when actuarially funded. There was, however, provision made to permit the company to change the formula or multiple under which the Special Sea Service Supplement was paid should the company at some future time improve the annuities provided by the Humble Annuity Plan.[7] This would not reduce the special supplement to the seagoing officer, but it could have the effect of so improving the annuities for the shoreside employees that the gap which had been established between seagoing officers and shoreside employees in Humble would be narrowed. This occurred later and became a source of confusion for the seagoing officers.

The main purpose of the Special Sea Service Retirement Annuity Supplement was to meet the demand of the JSTOA for a retirement plan that would recognize sea service as such. Since the company at the time was not prepared to go the full length of the industry "20-year, any-age" plan, this for the moment was a satisfactory substitute.

Satisfactory as this was, especially for those officers nearing 55, it did not meet the demands for a 20-year retirement. The association explained their position on this in the same *Bulletin* of November 15, 1966:

> In regard to the officers who would like a plan whereby they could retire after twenty years' service regardless of age, the Company told the Executive Committee that this can be done, but only by changing the basic Humble annuity plan around so as not to allow annuities to continue to build up based on an officer's age and service. Secondly, they maintain that other benefit plans, such as the Thrift Plan, might have to be changed to accomplish this. Thirdly, their contention is that all benefit plans, particularly pension plans, are aimed toward encouraging an officer to make his employment with Humble a career type of employment.
>
> We know that there are officers who do like the idea of being able to retire after twenty years' service regardless of age. Some of us on the Committee would like to do this too. However, we do not feel that we had the authority from the fleet as a whole to tamper with the existing basic annuity plan, or take away from any other benefit plan to bring this about.[8]

When the results of the association's efforts were presented to the membership, the company offer was approved overwhelmingly.

The vote was 121 to 15.[9] But again there was voter apathy. This appears to be a continuing problem for all democratically run organizations. There were more than 250 members in the JSTOA; less than half voted on this key issue. Perhaps the assumption that the offer was so attractive convinced many that their particular vote was not necessary.

Meanwhile, negotiations for other items had been taking place as part of the regular annual bargaining and the association was drawing a blank. On December 19, 1966, the executive committee brought the membership up to date with a six-page report on the negotiations, including the exchange of letters between the executive committee and the company. This exchange reflected the difficulty both sides faced in trying to reach an agreement. The letters were lengthy, but by that fact made clear how hard each side tries to argue the logic of its position in local-level bargaining.

Keeping everyone satisfied is never easy. There seemingly must be something for everyone, otherwise discontent develops. How to achieve this nice balance requires all the finesse and concern both sides can generate. It almost becomes a problem in distribution of the gains essentially agreed upon. In this particular bargaining a tremendous step forward had been taken to provide a pension for those age 55 or over, which was a distinct improvement over what was then available to shoreside employees. But to employees who are 25 or 35, age 55 seems almost out of sight; and some were certain that should they reach age 55, they would not still be at sea. This group wanted theirs now. For them a wage increase had top priority. Understandably, once the pension issue had been removed from the bargaining table, everyone would welcome a wage increase. But the association found itself facing a stone wall, despite increased compensation (not base wages) negotiated by national unions.

The explanatory *News Letter* of December 19, 1966 summarized the stalemate that had been reached between the association and the company.[10] National unions after an 80-day strike in 1965 had agreed to a settlement that had an estimated "cost" compounded for a four-year period of 30 per cent. It was the allocation of this 30 per cent that represented a real hurdle to the JSTOA bargaining committee, since almost all of it was directed by the national unions to improved pensions, higher payments for night relief officers, and increased overtime. The association included in its *News Letter* of December 19 the letter of December

5 to the "top management." In it the association challenged the company on their "no-wage-increase" stand:

> To return to our position regarding our desire, and we would suppose the Company's desire, to reach an amicable settlement, we call to your attention the fact that a relatively small company, namely, American Trading & Production Corporation, recently made a distinct improvement in their pension plan for licensed officers. This plan did not touch their basic pension plan except to improve upon it with respect to their licensed seagoing officers—and at no cost to any officer involved. And almost simultaneously they entered into negotiations for wage improvements which were in the area of between four and five per cent.
>
> For your further information the current base wage of these officers is higher than that for the officers in Humble and they have overtime, and they have 122 days of paid leave, and they have continuous service pay, *and* they carry four deck officers and four assistant engineers on every vessel.
>
> The Executive Committee of the JSTOA knows this and obviously are at a loss to understand why, particularly in these "high freight-rate times," Humble is so unrealistic as to believe it can tell this Executive Committee to go back to the fleet with nothing as far as money on the barrelhead is concerned.
>
> To say the pension plan is very costly is to say something that some believe and others disbelieve for the simple reason that it is next to impossible to put a price tag on this pension plan. As we said to the Company, time after time over the past four years, the purpose of the pension improvement in large measure was to provide an opportunity for that officer who desired to retire early to do so without a too substantial loss in retirement income. But no one knows how many officers, if any, will take advantage of this pension improvement. Furthermore, the cost of any pension improvement is certainly not paid for in any one year. It is spread out over many years. . . .[11]

In their reply the company repeated their position regarding wage increases, arguing that they already were ahead of their competition in this area and did not believe it to be wise to move out further. They also insisted that the recently negotiated sharply improved pension formula was not a substitute for other economic improvements.

> . . . First, we want to correct your understanding that it is the company's argument that the pension improvement which the association negotiated with the company is an offset to normal economic improvements. This is not true. The Special Sea Service

Retirement Annuity Supplement was negotiated as an improvement to meet the needs and desires of officers represented by the association. It is an improvement designed to leave Humble's basic benefit program unaltered. You tell us that the improvement has been very well received by your membership. This is a credit to our joint efforts.

You will recall that the association spent a great deal of time during the 1964 and 1965 contract negotiations trying to convince the company to divert wage increases to pension supplements. We did not agree that our wage compensation should be distorted by diverting wage increases to benefit improvements then. We continue to adhere to that principle.

This year the association presented proposals for wage increases in both your original proposals and your counter-proposals. Preparatory to our negotiations this fall our competitive position with respect to wages and other monetary compensation was analyzed. The analysis took into account the relatively minor compensation adjustments in national-union officer contracts as well as wage and other monetary improvements negotiated by independent unions representing officers employed by major oil companies. Based on our policy of paying among the leaders of competition we have concluded from the information used in our analysis that a wage increase for officers in the fleet cannot be justified at this time. . . .

While it is perhaps unnecessary, we want to reaffirm that the Marine Department's goal is to supply marine transportation for the company at competitive rates and most importantly at rates which preclude the possibility of a shift to alternate modes of oil transportation. Thus we are not willing to allow our compensation to get out of line with that of our competition. At the same time, we cannot allow compensation of our officers to get out of balance with officer compensation in the industry. To do so would result in dissatisfaction and the eventual loss of good, loyal employees. . . .[12]

The association replied briefly indicating its willingness to resume bargaining:

We are in receipt of your letter of December 12, 1966, in answer to our letter dated December 5, 1966.

We are ready and willing to resume negotiations with the Company at the earliest possible moment. We are prepared to substantiate our proposals for a wage increase and other adjustments in the agreement currently in effect between the Association and the Company.

We have no intention of moving away from our position that the manning of the *Esso Seattle* shall continue on a voluntary basis—unless, of course, the Company is willing to relieve the officers in accordance with the terms of the agreement, namely, 80 days on and 40 days off. Also, an additional officer should be had in both the Deck and Engine Departments.[13]

As a result of this correspondence, negotiations were resumed in the latter part of December 1966 but no progress was made. The difficulty continued to be the fact that national unions had taken their negotiated compensation—estimated as a 30 per cent cost to industry over 4 years—in improved pensions, increased payment to night relief officers (officers who are shore-based and who relieve seagoing officers when ships are in port), and higher overtime rates. There was nothing left for base wages. This is always a problem area. How can compensation negotiated by national unions and taken in fringe benefits be translated into a base wage that an independent union can argue is their due? Companies which have a wide range of fringe benefits maintain that national unions simply are catching up in this area. Since there had been no increase in base wages, Humble maintained they could not allow their base wage to become non-competitive. The JSTOA contended that the 30 per cent in labor costs, if taken as a base-wage increase, would come close to 7 per cent per year.

Whenever a base-wage increase is negotiated by independent unions, practically all fringe benefits, such as sick-leave pay, pensions, and life insurance, are increased automatically. To compare compensation diverted by national unions into fringes with what should be available on a cost basis as wage increases elsewhere is like comparing apples with apricots. Both are fruit—but the comparison ends there.

The company at this point offered to increase the overtime rate to $4.00 per hour effective November 1, 1966, and increase the company contribution toward hospitalization. It also insisted on assigning officers at its discretion to the *Esso Seattle* but were unwilling to relieve them for paid leave as were officers on vessels in domestic service—on the basis of 80 days on the vessel followed by 40 days of paid leave.

This proposal was rejected by the association. On January 24, 1967, the JSTOA negotiating committee proposed signing an amendment which would provide that overtime be increased to $4.23 per hour (a 48¢ increase) effective November 1, 1966; an hourly overtime rate for chief engineers of $8.24 for bunkering operations and where required to work with tools; the increase in company contribution to hospitalization as offered by the company; an increase in lodging allowance; and continued voluntary manning of the *Esso Seattle*; plus an agreement to meet on July 12, 1967 to negotiate further modification or amendments to the existing contract. This was not acceptable to the company.

Agreement, however, finally was reached on January 30, 1967. It provided for essentially what the association had proposed on January 24 except that the company would not agree to an hourly overtime-rate for the chief engineer. Instead they agreed to pay the chief engineer $25 a month while assigned to a vessel for "extra duties associated with bunkering operations." [14] The agreement was submitted to the membership and was approved by a vote of 119 to 44.[15]

In July of 1967, in accordance with the terms of that recently negotiated amendment to the agreement, the company and the association met for wage discussions. With little of the difficulty encountered in negotiations the previous fall and winter, agreement quickly was reached on a 6.2 per cent wage increase for all officers, to be effective July 12, 1967.[16] Recommended to the membership for ratification, it was approved by a substantial majority —161 to 23.[17]

Despite the fact that sharp gains in pensions, overtime rates, and base wages were being negotiated, the difficulties in reaching agreement seemed to grow. Whether this was due to a greater militancy shown by the JSTOA negotiating committee or a stiffening of its position by the company, is hard to say. Perhaps it was some of both. But there could be little doubt that bargaining with an independent union—at least this one—was no picnic. Nevertheless, agreement always was reached and, though the bargaining at times became bitter, there were no work stoppages or even threats of one.

NOTES

1. JSTOA, *News Letter,* August 11, 1965.
2. Telegram, JSTOA, to Joseph Andreae, Manager, Marine Department, Humble Oil and Refining Company, November 10, 1965.
3. JSTOA, *News Letter,* February 14, 1966.
4. JSTOA, *News Letter,* August 18, 1966.
5. JSTOA, *Bulletin,* November 15, 1966.
6. *Ibid.*
7. Memorandum of Understanding, JSTOA and Marine Department, Humble Oil and Refining Company, November 1, 1966.
8. JSTOA, *Bulletin,* November 15, 1966.

9. Certification of Results, Ratification Ballot, American Arbitration Association, December 10, 1966.

10. JSTOA, *News Letter,* December 19, 1966.

11. Letter, JSTOA to General Manager, Marine Department, Humble Oil and Refining Company, December 5, 1966.

12. Letter, Humble Oil Company to JSTOA, December 12, 1966.

13. Letter, JSTOA to General Manager, Marine Department, Humble Oil and Refining Company, December 14, 1966.

14. Memorandum of Understanding, JSTOA and Marine Department, Humble Oil and Refining Company, January 30, 1967.

15. Certification of Results, Ratification Ballot, American Arbitration Association, February 28, 1967.

16. Memorandum of Understanding, JSTOA and Marine Department, Humble Oil and Refining Company, July 12, 1967.

17. Certification of Results, Ratification Ballot, American Arbitration Association, August 15, 1967.

5
Difficulties But No Doubts

EACH INDEPENDENT UNION can tell its own story, its beginnings—quiet or hectic—its subsequent bargaining history, and the innumerable incidents that mark its internal maturity and its external stature. All have had their difficulties but none has had its doubts—so firm has been their foundation, so loyal their leadership.

In the summer of 1938 Cities Service deck and engineering officers formed their own union. They called it the Deepwater Officers Association (DOA). The reasons for its formation were similar to those advanced by officers in other major oil companies—the desire to be free from the entanglements associated with national unions, and not be required to participate in the "sit downs" and "quickies" that were all too frequent in the maritime industry during this period. The feelings of the fleet were expressed both orally and by letter:

> I want to belong to an association where my vote will carry some weight. I don't want to be forced to give up a job when I am perfectly satisfied with the money and working conditions, just because a few men in another organization are dissatisfied with their position.[1]
>
> As an independent union we will be free of entanglements in any difficulties between outside unions and other companies.[2]

In elections to determine what organization, if any, the officers in Cities Service desired to have represent them, the DOA was successful in both the deck department and the engine department. The deck department vote was 48 to 3; in the engine department it was 50 to 4. Following these elections the DOA was certified by the Labor Board as bargaining representative for all Cities Service officers.[3]

In subsequent years contracts were negotiated with the company and, although no pioneering was done, the association did keep abreast of prevailing wages and other changes in the East

Coast tanker industry. Essentially they patterned their agreements after those negotiated by other independent unions with other major oil companies such as Mobil, Texaco, and Esso. Certain tailor-made provisions, such as additional pay for length of service as an officer plus coverage by company-wide fringe benefits—a career pension, full sick-leave pay for extended periods, hospital–medical protection, and substantial life insurance—confirmed licensed officers in Cities Service in their belief that they were part of the Cities Service family. The independent union which they had formed guaranteed continuance of this relationship. Further proof of this was given when the company established a "Savings Plan" in which the licensed officers were invited to participate.

In post-World War II bargaining, the DOA followed the revolutionary 92-day vacation or paid-leave plan negotiated in Esso in 1946. For a trade-away of overtime, Cities Service officers made this substantial jump in vacations—from 30 days to 92 days. For a family man this longer vacation made up in some measure for the extended periods away from home that seagoing personnel traditionally must experience. These benefits, plus almost annual improvements in wages and other forms of compensation negotiated by the elected committees of the DOA, were achieved without the loss of a single day's wage to any officer because of a work stoppage. They were "never off pay" and the company's vessels never were delayed.

Despite these continued improvements, national unions always threatened. Efforts were made in 1958 and again in 1964 by the Marine Engineers Beneficial Association (MEBA) to secure the bargaining rights for engineers in the Cities Service fleet. Elections were held and the national union was unsuccessful. In 1964, however, the contest was close. The reason was twofold. The national union promised Cities Service engineers that their (MEBA's) extremely high initiation fee (between $1,000 and $2,000) would be waived if they signed a pledge card indicating support of the national union and an intention to vote for it; secondly, they held out the bait of a 20-year $300-a-month pension. This was especially attractive to the older and younger officers alike—the former for whom early retirement had been a long-sought goal; the latter, faster promotion resulting from the retirement of older officers, plus the knowledge that their required years at sea could be shortened at their option.

It was a fact that in 1964 national unions in the maritime industry had succeeded in negotiating 20-year pension plans under which an officer regardless of age could retire and receive approximately $300 per month. Major oil companies, and this included Cities Service, had overall company pensions predicated on a normal retirement age of 65 and a retirement income based on age, wage, and service. The DOA was in a difficult position to counter both the national union's promise to waive the initiation fee for Cities Service engineers and the expectation that, should that union win the election, all Cities Service officers presumably would participate in their attractive early-retirement arrangement.

Since the company would not at this time promise to match the national-union pension, the outcome of any election between the national union and the independent seemed bleak indeed for the independent. Despite this, however, the MEBA failed to dislodge the DOA in the two elections (the first was inconclusive) conducted by the American Arbitration Association[4] (licensed officers were supervisors under Taft-Hartley, which made the services of the National Labor Relations Board, for election purposes, unavailable). The DOA considered the results both a moral and a real victory since the odds in favor of the MEBA's winning had become so tremendous. The fact of the 20-year pension, which the national union had secured, had become a very large carrot dangled before Cities Service engineers. This almost won them the election.

But there was another side to the coin. The Cities Service fleet was a closely knit group. Relations between management ashore and the officers on the ships were on a first-name basis. All the port representatives (shore-based management who visited the ships to learn at first hand of the needs of the officers and at the same time deliver the company's messages) had themselves been seagoing officers in Cities Service. This tightly knit shoreside and seagoing relationship was poignantly demonstrated on those occasions where there was a death of either a member of the shoreside management or a seagoing officer. From far and near representatives from both groups and their wives came to pay their respects. The author witnessed several of these occasions, and the evidence of the bonds that joined the members of the Cities Service family made a lasting impression.

Because ships were offshore and the first election was inconclusive, the total time taken for the two elections consumed the better part of two years. Back at the bargaining table in the spring of 1966, the negotiating team representing the DOA made up for lost time and reached agreement with the company that provided substantial improvement in wages, overtime, and other benefits. The membership ratified this agreement with an enthusiastic 59 to 11 vote.[5]

But the 20-year pension was not bargained in the 1966 negotiations. This had to wait until some ice was broken by independent unions elsewhere in the tanker industry. When it happened in Mobil and later in Texaco, Exxon, and Getty, Cities Service was ready to move in the same direction. The pension program became effective January 1, 1970.[6] The payment formula was almost identical with other 20-year, no-age plans in the maritime industry for licensed officers. It guaranteed a minimum of $325 per month, or 32.5% of the "final average" pay, whichever is the higher.

By definition of "final average pay" as the average of the officer's highest basic earnings for any consecutive 60 months of the last 120 months of credited service preceding his retirement, officers in the upper categories—i.e., chief mate and first assistant engineer—could retire with amounts well above the $325 minimum—and the monies are *payable for life*. What was equally important, the officers continued to be covered by all the regular company benefit-plans, including the savings plan.

As in the case of other independent unions in the major oil company tanker fleets, negotiating a 20-year, no-age pension took considerable persuading of shore-based management, but it was done. Today there still is some head-shaking among shoreside management about the wisdom and the financial soundness of such departures from the tried, trusted, and funded company-wide retirement plans. Some indication of how wobbly some of these "early retirement" plans are was the sheer necessity during the 1972 bargaining, for the National Maritime Union representing seamen on the East and Gulf Coasts, to move the minimum age for a 20-year pension to 55. With the lay-up or sale of all American-flag passenger ships plus a large number of dry-cargo vessels, the liability left for pension payments to members of the National Maritime Union became the responsibility of those companies still operating. They would have to generate the income necessary to meet this annual multi-million-dollar pension obligation. To do so would have bankrupted some without solving the pension dilemma. The moment of truth had come; and not a moment too soon. Payments to those retired could not be continued if the rate at which the money was being generated did not increase. With a decreasing merchant fleet this was not possible. The formula had to be changed.

Finally, companies bargaining with the National Maritime Union agreed to meet the responsibility of paying pensions to those already retired as well as to those who would retire in the future—but only on the condition that the pension formula be revised to become more realistic financially. A move in this direction was the establishment of a minimum age of 55 before pension payments could begin. Whether or not this substantial change will be sufficient to satisfy the actuarial requirements for a properly funded pension only time will tell. But the National Maritime Union experience is sufficiently sobering to recognize that it takes more than political popularity and clout to make a pension work. In this instance the huge hoax that would have been perpetrated on the unsuspecting national-union members relying on promised pensions was narrowly averted by the insistence on the part of the companies bargaining with the National Maritime Union that sound pension-practices be established.

Despite the fact that the 1969 negotiations in the maritime industry resulted in the largest money package ever negotiated for a three-year period in the history of the industry (affecting both those represented by national unions and those represented by independent unions), by 1972 there were new demands made with the same insistence that always accompanies demands—i.e., that the negotiating committee *must* get this or that. What was negotiated yesterday is as forgotten as Thanksgiving turkey on Easter Sunday. This attitude of "what have you done for me lately?" and "what are you going to do for me now?" is as normal as a soldier's griping. If it did not happen, then something really is wrong. But some managements become visibly upset when proposals or demands are made by the employees' bargaining team that are clearly impossible to grant. This is unfortunate because sometimes it affects the mood for negotiations, causing the company to assume a negative posture. This does not happen where the company bargaining team is mature and experienced.

Bargaining is a sifting process and, although it is the duty of the employee representative at least to present *all* the views of *all* his constituents, this does not mean that he is so immature as to believe they are all bargainable in the sense that firm positions will be taken on each and every one of them. It is the obligation of the elected representative to use his *judgment* to determine what is *possible* at the time. That is why he is elected by his fellow-employees.

Edmund Burke was elected to the House of Commons from

the city of Bristol in November 1774. In a speech to his constituents he summed up relations of a representative and his constituents for all time. While elected representatives to local-level bargaining committees or independent unions may be far from Burke in time, geography, and the matters at hand, an excerpt from his speech will show that the principle of representation is as true now as it was on the day Burke made his remarks to his constituents:

> Certainly, Gentlemen, it ought to be the happiness and glory of a representative to live in the strictest union, the closest correspondence, and the most unreserved communication with his constituents. Their wishes ought to have great weight with him, their opinions high respect; their business unremitted action. It is his duty to sacrifice his repose, his satisfactions, to theirs—and above all, ever and in all cases, to prefer their interest to his own.
>
> But his unbiased opinion, his mature judgement, his enlightened conscience, he ought not to sacrifice to you, to any man, or to any set of men living. These he does not derive from your pleasure—no nor from the law and the Constitution. They are a trust from Providence, for the abuse of which he is deeply answerable. Your representative owes you, not his industry only, but his judgement; and he betrays instead of serving you, if he sacrifices it to your opinion.[7]

These eloquent words, evincing the highest service an elected representative can perform for his constituents, are applicable to any elected official, anywhere, anytime. In local-level bargaining they are most apt to be carried out, not because representatives of local bargaining units are by their nature superior beings or more altruistically oriented than representatives of major national unions, but because the restricted area of local-level bargaining almost makes it mandatory that the *common* interests be served—and this is best done by the use of the elected representative's judgment.

Which brings us to a most difficult question—what constitutes "common interests"? Probably a rule-of-thumb definition would be: a strong and almost universal desire for something which, either by a trade or by simple acquiescence, can be bargained by management and the local bargaining unit, and continue the company sufficiently viable to achieve its goal in the marketplace. In short, is it economically feasible?

An example of something that was bargained and served the common interests" was the revolutionary system of paid leave or vacations which the JSTOA negotiated with the Standard Oil Company of New Jersey in 1946. As a result of these negotiations, officers, instead of continuing to receive 30 days of vacation each year, now would be entitled to *three* 30-day vacations in each year. But in reaching this agreement some trading was done—overtime and port relief as they then existed were eliminated. Both of these had proved burdensome administratively, as well as costly, and the company was prepared to give something in return for their elimination. The officers in turn were desirous of more time at home. By the agreement reached, therefore, the "common interests" of both the employees and the management were served, and the company also was served in that it achieved more efficient operations.

Today the demand for more leisure time is universal, and it is no wonder, then, that men going to sea are demanding more time ashore. Today the average seagoing officer, at least on tankers, earns 16 days of paid leave for each 30 that he works—or a total of 128 days a year.* But it is still not enough—if one were to read the minutes of meetings held aboard ships of the various companies. Nor is this demand new. As early as 1964 and 1965 this proposal began to show up in the correspondence between the members and their elected representatives, and it has been a priority proposal among those made by several independent unions for several years. It is easy for shoreside people to look with amazement bordering on annoyance at a proposal of one day vacation for each day worked; but when it is realized that the person who works ashore receives an average of 3 weeks' vacation each year plus approximately 10 holidays, plus every Saturday and Sunday—not to mention his free time generally after 4 or 5 P.M. —a "one for one" proposal by ships' officers hardly seems unreasonable. A recent letter from a captain, concurred in by the chief engineer, on a Cities Service ship is typical of the increased pressure on the company for more paid leave or vacation—*because of the increased pressure on the officers.*

ss *C. S. Norfolk*
Boston, Massachusetts
November 9, 1972

Dear Sir:

The Deepwater Officers Association wage and contract negotia-

---

* As a result of negotiations in 1973, paid leave has become 17 days for each 30 worked.

tions with Cities Service Tankers Corporation will be held in November or December of this year, I understand. I wish at this time to express my views on what should be negotiated for the masters and chief engineers. I believe, most emphatically, that the union and company should agree to three months' work and three months' paid leave. Work six months a year, receive vacation with pay six months a year. This to be paid without a reduction in our regular pay. Due to the Wage Board's refusal to grant pay raises over a given non-inflationary per cent and the huge amounts of overtime being paid first assistants and chief mates, who are making more money than the masters and chief engineers the past three years without the ultimate responsibilities, I feel this is the only satisfactory settlement possible. I know I am very dissatisfied with the present wage set-up.

The new SIU contract agreed to by the company with the numerous overtime rates and conflicts make the master's job more demanding than ever.

Increased pressures about water and air pollution from oil and smoke also add to the woes of the master's and chief engineer's job.

Old-age problems with the ships increase job pressures more and more each year.

Due to these three reasons alone, I find that in order to maintain some semblance of sanity, what's left of it, six months' work a year is about all I can stand in the capacity of master aboard ship.

Yours truly,
R. BRIDGEO, *Master*

I concur with the above remarks of Captain Bridgeo. The "one for one" plan seems to be the most reasonable and just solution to the increasingly inequitable situation of the captain and chief engineer.

FRANCIS CROWLEY
Chief Engineer[8]

The letter stresses the problem of the master and the chief engineer on a deteriorating vessel and the new surveillance of the water and the air by the Coast Guard and others to detect pollution. This has increased the tension of these senior officers. But there is an equally strong demand for additional vacation from the other officers. The answer is not yet on the horizon, but, based on the solutions of past serious problems, this too will be solved—by patience and persistence, and with due regard to the "common interests."

In 1969 it was possible because of the nature of their trade for

Reynolds Metals Co., which operates two American-flag ships, to negotiate a break in the pattern of one day of paid leave for each two days worked. Without detailing the give and take which made this possible, the net result as far as additional paid leave is concerned was an agreement reached with the American Licensed Officers Association that provided for paid leave on the basis of one day of paid leave for each day-and-one-half worked.[9] Because the ALOA (the independent union representing these officers) was not bound by a national-union wage or paid-leave pattern, they were free to negotiate that which was desired by their membership and feasible for the company to establish.

Although the perennial plea for more time at home may not at the moment be met in a manner satisfactory to everyone, further progress has been made, but again affecting very few. The move in this direction occurred in April 1973. The bargaining that took place between the Ingram Seagoing Officers Association (Ind.) and Ingram Ocean Systems resulted in the first "one for one" vacation or paid-leave arrangement for deep-sea officers in the maritime industry. It became effective May 1, 1973, after unanimous approval by the ISOA membership.[10] This long-sought goal of maritime labor organizations, admittedly, was gained by a small independent union whose membership includes only those employed aboard the two ocean-going barges of the Ingram Company. Although these vessels, combination tug-barges, carry more cargo than the traditional East Coast tanker and trade in the same areas—between Gulf ports and ports north of Hatteras—their crew size is considerably smaller than the conventional tanker, 14 *versus* 30 or more. On the other hand, the tug-barge concept does not compare competitively with the conventional tanker in speed or "port turnaround"; so that the ability to bargain a "one for one" paid leave arrangement was not necessarily predicated on a cost edge over their competition.

When the "one for one" proposal first was made by the ISOA negotiating committee, it was agreed to by the company with the proviso that *all overtime* be eliminated. This, however, was not acceptable to the committee. The company then offered improvements in wages, overtime rates, and vacation in the existing agreement. Their offer was similar to the response given by major oil companies when "one for one" proposals were made to them by the various independent-union negotiating committees. These improvements in their existing agreement were accepted by the ISOA negotiating committee, subject to membership approval. However, when the company's offer was presented to the membership it was turned down. The committee was instructed by the membership to pursue the "one for one" paid leave objective but without sacrificing overtime for work performed in excess of 8 hours per day.

After further discussions between the bargaining committee and the company, another offer was made by the company which provided for a "one for one" paid-leave plan *and* for the payment of overtime for work performed in excess of 8 hours in any one day. To achieve this, slight reductions in base pay were agreed to by the bargaining committee. When this revised agreement was submitted to the membership it was ratified unanimously. This would appear to prove that time at home is more important than money. Essentially the same arrangement was negotiated by the unlicensed personnel represented by the Ingram Seamens Association (Ind.).

Mention should be made here of the importance of overtime to employees. Overtime represents not merely compensation but protection. It has a monitoring effect on overzealous supervisors who can find all manner of "reasons" for working employees beyond their allotted time where overtime does not have to be paid for such work. The payment of overtime tempers their zeal.

For shore-based industry the Wages and Hours Act mandates payment at time-and-one-half for work in excess of 40 hours per week. The maritime industry is exempt from the provisions of the Wages and Hours Act. Payment for work in excess of 8 hours in any one day or in excess of 40 hours per week is a negotiable item. Parties to a labor agreement, where overtime has been agreed to previously, can negotiate a "changee for changee" that could result in trading away such overtime for additional vacation. This had been done in the Esso negotiations in 1946 when the parties negotiated a "one for three" vacation or "paid leave" plan. This provided for the elimination of *all* overtime. It was not until the 1960 Esso–JSTOA agreement that an overtime rate again was negotiated for work in excess of 8 hours in any one day.

There is general agreement that, where employees are required to work in excess of 8 hours without the payment of overtime, there is grousing and misunderstanding despite (in this instance) the benefit bargained in exchange—substantial additional vacation. This was why in Texaco and Mobil the extended-vacation agreements were modified in 1947 by providing fewer days of vacation per year than the Esso agreement called for; but the principle of paying overtime for work in excess of 8 hours was retained.

Thus the retention of overtime in the Ingram agreement *and* the gaining of a "one for one" vacation was a significant breakthrough. It represented a crack in the armor of resistance to this concept by those companies operating deep-sea tanker fleets. This paid-leave pattern as negotiated in Ingram may or may not be followed by others in the maritime industry, or it may be negotiated in a modified form. But surely it will be mentioned across the table in future bargaining. That this "first" was achieved without fanfare or work stoppage is typical of the tailor-made agreements negotiated by bargaining on the local level—and all within the framework of what is economically feasible.

NOTES

1. Letter, Charles Heath, 3rd Mate, M.S. *Cities Service Ohio,* November 2, 1938.
2. Letter, Captain N. Nelander, s.s. *Hagwood,* November 21, 1938.
3. *Decisions and Orders,* National Labor Relations Board, Vol. X, p. 825.
4. Certification of Results, Representation election, DOA *vs.* MEBA, American Arbitration Association, January 12, 1965.
5. DOA, *News Letter,* May 13, 1966.
6. Agreement, DOA and Cities Service Tankers Corp., January 1, 1970.
7. *Burke's Politics,* edd. Ross J. S. Hoffman and A. Paul Levack, (New York: Knopf, 1949), p. 115.
8. Letter, s.s. *Cities Service Norfolk* to DOA, November 9, 1972.
9. Agreement, ALOA and Reynolds Metals Company, October 17, 1969.
10. Agreement, ISOA and Ingram Ocean Systems, May 1, 1973.

6

The Role of the Executive Committee

IN BARGAINING, the seriousness of the issues and the positions taken by each side do not vary regardless of the union doing the bargaining—independent or national—except that normally where independent unions bargain the "climate" is somewhat friendlier. The difficulties to be faced depend on the particular issues involved and the parties doing the bargaining. If the matter at hand is substantial in the minds of the representatives of the union and if their constituents are expecting positive results and will not take no for an answer, their efforts will be directed almost passionately to securing these results. If, on the other hand, the management has a firm policy with respect to certain items and under no circumstances, based on past experience, seems willing to move, bargaining can be bitter. And if either management and union representatives, or both of them, are abrasive, the difficulty in reaching agreement is compounded.

In these situations an independent union undergoes the test of fire. A case in point was the bargaining that took place in the fall of 1967 between the JSTOA and the marine management of the Humble Oil and Refining Company (now Exxon). Agreement was not reached until December of the following year. The executive committee of the association during that period was extremely active. In the previous year a dispute had arisen among the members of the executive committee wherein one member believed that the other three were too impatient and were not fully appreciative of the successful efforts of former executive committees in negotiating agreements. The majority, in turn, believed the agreements previously negotiated had not spelled out working rules in a sufficiently precise manner. The issue that prompted this polarization involved the right of the executive committee, without previous authorization from the membership, to terminate an agreement which contained an automatic renewal clause.

Over the years agreements made between the JSTOA and

Humble, together with its predecessors—Esso Shipping, Standard Oil of New Jersey (essentially the same employer)—had continued on a year-to-year basis with negotiations taking place each year for a modification of the existing agreement. While each party had the right to terminate the agreement by notification to the other 60 days prior to the anniversary date, neither the association nor the company ever had exercised this option. The majority of the executive committee in 1967–68 believed that the committee would have greater bargaining strength if they could come down to the wire, as it were, with the current agreement about to expire.

This, of course, becomes a matter of philosophy. Is a group, especially an independent group, in a better bargaining position to begin negotiations with a fixed date terminating the current agreement? The answer really depends on how interested both parties are in having an agreement, and what can be gained and what can be lost by either party if the current agreement terminates before agreement for a new one is reached. There is no hard-and-fast answer to this kind of question. Perhaps simplistically speaking it could be said to boil down to "good faith" on the part of the union and management.

The author has participated in negotiations where traditionally the agreement automatically terminated at a fixed date. In cases where bargaining had not resulted in reaching an agreement by the termination date, the parties mutually extended the existing agreement in 30-day periods with the understanding that when agreement was reached it would become retroactive to the date at which the previous agreement had terminated. Much has to do with the "climate" in which the bargaining is taking place. If it appears that the parties will reach agreement, the delay is of no consequence. And in these instances, termination neither strengthened nor weakened the position of either party.

Since the 1966 agreement between the company and the JSTOA had not been terminated by either party, the question of extending the existing contract by mutual agreement was academic. For the most part the membership assumed this condition would continue to prevail, since the issue never had been raised in a serious manner. Furthermore, one member of the committee believed any action by the executive committee to terminate the agreement should have prior membership approval. The JSTOA's constitution said nothing about this. The member who believed prior membership approval should be had, before the executive committee took action to terminate, persuaded a sufficient number of members to initiate an amendment to the JSTOA constitution to accomplish this. The amendment ballot read as follows:

> TERMINATION OF AGREEMENT: Any agreement in effect between the Jersey Standard Tanker Officers Association and the company shall not be terminated by any Executive Committee, unless, at least 90 days prior to the time called for in the Agreement to notify the company of the desire to terminate, namely 60 days, the membership has been given an opportunity by secret ballot to vote yes or no on such proposed termination. Ballots in such a referendum shall be forwarded to the American Arbitration Association, or similar organization, for opening and counting.[1]

The 1967–68 negotiations with the company were lengthy. Begun in the fall of 1967 after months of bargaining which was unusually acrimonious, talks were recessed in March, 1968, when no agreement was reached. A prime issue was the 20-year pension which already was in effect in that portion of the industry where national unions did the bargaining. Also uppermost in the minds of the members of the executive committee was a demand on the company that a "manning" scale be written into the agreement. The company consistently had refused to bargain "manning" in the sense that they would be compelled by agreement to carry more officers on their vessels than, in their judgment as managers, were necessary. This had become a serious issue—especially since by the terms of agreements negotiated by national unions a manning scale had been negotiated. The majority of the JSTOA executive committee believed that, based on comparison and need, additional officers should be required on every vessel.

The Coast Guard has a requirement that three mates and three engineers on each vessel cover the 24-hour period for each department. Each of these officers stands two watches per day of four hours each. In addition to the watchstanding officers there is a master and a chief engineer. However, national unions representing seagoing officers had negotiated a manning scale which required that four deck officers and four assistant engineers be carried. The extra engineer and extra mate were considered "day workers." Where the vessel sailed without either of these extra officers, the wages of the missing officer were, until recently, divided among the remaining officers. By the terms of the 1972 Masters, Mates and Pilots (AFL–CIO) agreement, these wages now are paid "to an MM&P Special Pension or Welfare Fund."[2] Obviously "manning" is a basic issue because it involves the number of people required to do the job.

On Humble ships the company's practice had been to place an additional mate and/or engineer on those vessels where the company believed they were necessary. In Texaco no additional officers, other than those required by Coast Guard manning rules, are carried. In the ordinary operation of a vessel where three mates and three assistant engineers are employed there is considerable overtime. This is a factor, at least in Texaco, as far as membership demands for additional officers are concerned. The addition of an officer would result in reducing the earnings of the watchstanding officers. To national unions the requirement that additional officers be carried means more union members. This was of paramount concern to them.

The whole question of manning was also involved in the broader area of automation. The number of unlicensed personnel on Humble ships had been reduced sharply on the basis that, with automated equipment installed in their vessels, the same number of unlicensed personnel was not necessary. The officers, however, especially the engineers, argued that greater burdens and responsibilities were placed on them because of the reduction in engine-room personnel. The question of how many individuals are required where there has been a certain amount of automation is a bitterly debated issue in practically all current bargaining, whether it be related to ships, railroads, factories, or steel plants.

The majority of the JSTOA executive committee believed that the bargaining position of the association on this question would have been stronger had they notified the company, in accordance with the terms of the agreement, that they wished to terminate the agreement at its normal expiration date. They were angry at the company's continued refusal to write a manning scale into the agreement and felt impotent to do anything to change the company's mind in the light of the automatic continuation of the existing agreement. The member who differed with the majority felt equally strongly that the termination of the agreement would have made little difference in the actual negotiations—unless the association were prepared to implement their position by calling a strike over the issue of manning. If any event, he believed, the executive committee should seek approval from the membership in advance of any drastic action that could lead the association down the path to possible affiliation with a national union before the membership was fully aware of what was happening.

Letters were written which included minority and majority reports on the question of terminating the agreement. The minority report was prepared by the member of the committee who had recommended an amendment giving the membership an opportunity to vote on whether or not an agreement should be terminated prior to its anniversary date. The majority report was written by the 3 members who felt that when an executive committee is elected they have broad responsibilities and must make judgments which, in their opinion, ultimately are in the best interest of the membership. Clearly a matter of policy was involved, as excerpts from the minority and majority reports will bear out.

MAJORITY REPORT

The majority of your Committee after meeting with our fellow officers, believed that we had to terminate the contract and all future contracts on their termination date to close this door that the Company has been using to gain their ends at the bargaining table. In conscience, this can help or hinder you as an officer in our fight for better conditions. *This notice of termination is common practice in the majority of all union contracts.* Why has our dissenting member been circulating all these scare tactics and throwing up roadblocks at our every turn while we are trying to give you officers the strongest representation? We are fighting for you officers each and every one of you from the Master and Chief down. Not one of the majority on this Committee has any ax to grind. What we are fighting for is what we, after meeting and talking to you officers, feel is right and just and using the national contracts as a basis of comparison.

Had this termination clause in our contract been a detriment to the Company they would have tried to get it removed from the contract years ago. *They have not: Why not?* Because this has been a tool for their benefit and they have used it. Let's get the termination clause and the rest of the loopholes out of our contract that only benefit the Company.

FRANK STODDARD
JOHN MURPHY
DWAINE HETTINGER

MINORITY REPORT

If the contract is terminated the Company and the Association can go their separate ways. There will be no obligation *under law* for the Company to bargain. We *might* be better off without an agreement—but *we could be worse off*. Although in bargaining you always have difficulty with the Company negotiating wages and overtime increases and other improvements, we have been

> able to do this and the membership has ratified these agreements —and we have held on to what we had obtained in the past because these were *guaranteed* and *secured* by a continuing agreement.
>
> Who pioneered paid leave; who negotiated continuous service pay and *increased* it? Not any national union, not the Company, but the *JSTOA*. And these improvements were secured while we had a continuing agreement so that no officer had to give up anything or bargain away anything, or worry about losing gains negotiated previously.
>
> Believe me, this is a serious situation—serious for *all of us*. If through my insistence on writing my minority report, I forced the majority to give you your right to vote yes or no on terminating the contract, I feel that I have done my duty. No man is infallible and, in my opinion, *no three men* should presume to speak for all. Either this is a democratically run organization or it is a tool for a few. I believe it should be run democratically—even if this means my fellow-members on the Executive Committee accuse me of selling the fleet down the river.
>
> JOHN MCSHANE[3]

In the balloting the minority position was upheld by the membership. The vote was 69 to 60 *to approve* the amendment to require the executive committee to have prior approval from the membership before terminating an agreement. The balloting was conducted by the American Arbitration Association.[4]

During this period fruitless negotiations with the company were continuing. The company persisted in refusing to write a manning scale into the agreement and difficulties still remained in reaching agreement on the 20-year, any-age, seagoing retirement plan. In a lengthy report to the membership, after the parties had reached an impasse in March, the executive committee asked for:

> comment from the fleet by letter, telegram or radio on the major portions in the negotiations on which we have reached an impasse with the company, namely:
>
> 1. The right to use the Merchant Mariner's Document if early retirement is accepted [the 20-year plan].
> 2. The amount of the pension and failure by the Company to offer credit for unlicensed sea service.
> 3. The amounts and effective date of the Company wage offer.
> 4. Working conditions.[5]

A burning issue with the majority of the executive committee was the right of an officer to retain his Merchant Mariner's Document (issued by the U. S. Coast Guard—and necessary to sail) should he retire under the proposed 20-year pension plan. Members of national unions were, by their agreement with industry, required to surrender theirs. The company maintained that they should not be asked to do more than industry did in this 20-year pension matter—especially since they did not agree with the philosophy of a 20-year pension in the first place. But the association held firm.

Negotiations (after the March recess in bargaining) did not resume until July 25, 1968. Despite the long hiatus, however, early agreement was not in the cards. Among other issues, the 20-year pension remained unresolved. Since there was little likelihood of agreement being reached, negotiations again were suspended. Resumed in the fall of 1968, some progress was made, although the executive committee continued to insist that specific working rules be written into the agreement as to what an officer should and should not do. The company continued to refuse, asserting that the officer was a "working supervisor": he was expected to use judgment in determining what should or should not be done.

Agreement finally was reached on December 19, 1968 after more than a year of bargaining. According to its terms there would be a 4.2 per cent wage increase retroactive to November 1, 1967; plus $52 per month additional for each officer retroactive to August 1, 1968; plus improvements in overtime, transportation, and the company contribution to the hospital–medical–surgical plan, and, as well, a 20-year pension plan (without the necessity to give up either the company-wide career pension or the special seagoing supplement to pensions negotiated in 1967).[6]

Despite achieving wage, overtime, and other gains (especially the 20-year pension), the executive committee recommended that the agreement *not be approved*. Failure to reach agreement on "working rules" and a manning scale irked the negotiating committee, and caused their negative position on ratification. The member of the executive committee who earlier had disagreed with the majority on the right of the executive committee to terminate an agreement without prior membership approval was defeated when he ran for re-election. The no-approval position taken by the executive committee therefore was unanimous. It was set forth in a bold heading in the association's *News Letter* of January 8, 1969 which read:

Your executive committee strongly urges the membership not to approve the contract now up for ratification. Join together and make your vote an effective weapon and a united protest to this Humble offer that is so grossly lacking in benefits that are already enjoyed by our counterparts in the national unions.

We would like to make it crystal clear to all concerned, so that there will be no false impressions, that because the executive committee signed this contract we recommend it. This was the only avenue that could be used to bring this contract to the fleet for your vote.[7]

Despite the strong support of the executive committee by the membership in practically all of its dealings with the company, and further, in the face of the *News Letter* recommending that the membership turn down the agreement, by a close vote the membership *approved* the agreement. The tally was 124 to 111, as announced by the American Arbitration Association.[8] The vote for approving the agreement was all the more remarkable since, on the same ballot, the membership by a vote of 159 to 75 followed the recommendation of the executive committee that they reverse their vote of the previous year requiring prior membership approval to terminate the contract.[9] The earlier vote had been 69 to 60 to require membership approval.

This is interesting and it seems to tell us that, although in this instance the membership encouraged the executive committee in their demands for certain items such as manning and spelled-out working conditions, these apparently were not of sufficient importance when they were not achieved to cause the membership to postpone approval of monetary gains, plus the 20-year pension that had been won in the course of the negotiations. It could be said that the membership made a mistake in approving the agreement—at least this was the belief of the executive committee. On the other hand, the virtue of democratic procedure is that the individual is given the opportunity to make his own determination in a matter of vital interest to himself. What other yardstick would one suggest?

To permit any executive committee to take the full burden of the final decision upon itself would go a long way toward creating a power mechanism which—although on occasion it might do good—because of such concentration of power in the hands of a few could readily result in irreparable economic and other damage. An executive committee of any union does and should have broad powers to negotiate agreements; and it is presumed they do negotiate the best agreements possible at the time. But to insure membership control, all agreements should be subject to ratification. The case just mentioned is unusual in that the executive committee itself was not happy with the results of its own bargaining and was frank enough to say so. On the other hand, the membership apparently was not so wedded to certain demands made by the executive committee as to turn down the entire agreement because these were not secured. On the other hand, the vote to give the executive committee the authority to terminate an agreement could be considered a procedural matter and of no immediate economic consequence. Adherence to the executive committee's recommendations in this latter area was understandable, since it involved no financial loss. But when a matter of dollars and cents, with considerable retroactivity, was involved, plus the long-sought-for 20-year pension, it was a different story. In a headcount, money on the barrel-head generally wins out over less tangible items. This is a political fact of life.

The more frequent case where differences develop between a negotiating committee and the rank and file of the membership occurs when the negotiating committee bargains the best agreement it can and submits it to the membership for their final judgment either enthusiastically recommending its approval, or saying little about it but certainly not recommending that it *not* be approved, and the membership disapproves it. This happened in Texaco when in the fall of 1969 the executive committee negotiated substantial improvements for all the officers which the membership nevertheless turned down. Here was a case where the executive committee although not enthusiastic with the results of their bargaining efforts reported those results in an approving manner to the membership. The TTOA *News Letter* of November 22, 1969 can hardly be called negative:

> In one of the most hectic and grueling negotiations ever to take place between the TTOA and Texaco, the six-member Executive Committee and Association Adviser negotiated night and day for almost eight days and reached the Agreement which is enclosed and is submitted to all the members in good standing for their approval or disapproval. We would be less than honest if we did not admit deep disappointment in not achieving the "one for one" which practically all the officers would like to have. However, the Company was determined not to move out in front as far as the granting of additional paid leave was concerned. There were many reasons offered for their position. First and foremost

among these was the alleged tremendous cost. "One for one" meant adding 60 days to the 122 that currently exist. However, every day and every night the association continued to argue heatedly and, we believe, logically, for the additional paid leave. But without success.

What we did negotiate, we believe, is a tremendous money package. We will not cover in detail in this report the areas that will provide more money for all officers; an examination of the Memorandum of Understanding by the membership will indicate quickly that in addition to the 6% increase in base wages, the new overtime rate (*which is higher than the industry rate*) will in itself generate considerable additional money for watchstanding officers. Further, the payment of overtime for Saturday at sea will result in further substantial money income. The length of service increases establishes a new pattern, plus more money. The latter is one of the really great achievements of these negotiations. You will note that the LOSI [length of service increment] has not only been increased for the first five years to $10 per month for each year but will be payable *each year* rather than at intervals of more than a year as is currently done. Also, the Master and Chief Engineer *will not lose* LOSI previously earned as a Mate or Assistant Engineer.

The elimination of the 72 hours for port time, and the requirement that the vessel be "loading or discharging cargo," will provide additional income for watchstanding officers. Also, note the changes in the shifting ship clause and the port time clause. These will eliminate many of the disputes that previously arose and will result in added compensation for watchstanding officers.

The Master and Chief Engineer, apart from the 6% increase in base wages, will receive an addendum of $250 per month. This will be paid while on the ship, while on standby, and *while on paid leave*. In other words it will be payable for the full 12 months of the year. This amount is considerably more than the Company first offered and was gained only after heated debate that lasted many hours.[10]

Despite this generally favorable report by the executive committee and their recommendation for an affirmative vote, the agreement was defeated. The vote was 102 against, 84 in favor.[11] The issue most bothersome to the officers—despite the substantial improvements that were negotiated—was a slight downward change in the transportation clause. In Texaco, as in the other major oil companies where independent unions represent the licensed officers, officers going on vacation, as they do two or three times a year, are paid transportation either all the way or part of the way from the ship to their home; and return to the ship. There are various formulas in the different agreements covering this item. In Texaco, prior to the 1969 negotiations, transportation had been first-class air transportation. In the 1969 negotiations the company had agreed to extend the distance for which they would be responsible to pay transportation, but insisted that air transportation become economy class.

That this issue was the primary one causing the members to turn down the agreement became clear as minutes from ships' meetings were received. In a *News Letter* dated January 26, 1970, reporting to the membership on meetings between the executive committee and the company held on January 19, following the rejection of the earlier Memorandum of Understanding the association reported:

> The general consensus of these meetings, and the overall desire of the fleet, was to submit the Memorandum of Understanding again to the membership for their approval or disapproval. However, before submitting such a Memorandum again to the fleet the Association had a mandate from the fleet to seek to take care of those items which it was felt had been the basis for the rejection of this Memorandum. Primary among the objections to the existing Memorandum was the matter of transportation. Despite the fact that additional transportation was secured, that is, transportation was extended beyond the current zones thereby benefiting officers who were not receiving such transportation heretofore, the fact that to achieve this the Association had to agree to relinquish first-class transportation as it currently prevails caused great resentment in the fleet. All manner of remarks have been made regarding this loss of first-class transportation and the Association's Committee therefore knew that this was a matter of concern to practically all the officers and one that they felt they must attend to during these meetings.[12]

As a result of the subsequent meetings between the association and the company following the rejection of the first agreement, the company agreed to modify the Memorandum of Understanding in the matter of transportation. This was reported to the membership:

> About eight o'clock on the evening of January 19, after arguing with the Association all day, the Company caucaused. Upon their return they agreed to pay first-class transportation where this is referred to in the Memorandum of Understanding. In other words, the improved transportation as far as its *being extended beyond existing zones* will stay in the agreement and all transportation will be *first class*. The effective date, if the Memoran-

dum is ratified, will be December 26, 1969. The Company stated that they will make no other changes in the Memorandum of Understanding negotiated last fall.[13]

These cases are cited not because they are the only times when difficulties arise in bargaining but rather to emphasize the human equation in bargaining. In the first case (JSTOA) a militant executive committee did not believe that what it signed was adequate, and recommended its rejection. And the membership responded by approving the agreement. In the second case (TTOA) an equally militant executive committee negotiated substantial improvements but, because one of these improvements was in the nature of a "trade-off" in the area of transportation (an extension of the distances to which transportation would be paid in exchange for having all transportation become economy class rather than first class), the agreement was turned down by the membership, although the executive committee had recommended approval.

It should be pointed out that the latter case was a clear victory for the association; but it was risky since there was a strong possibility that the company would insist on making the effective date of the Memorandum of Understanding February 1, 1970, rather than the retroactive date of September 1, 1969. However, the company did not seek to penalize the association, and, through it, the membership, for the delay in reaching an agreement satisfactory to the membership.

This was but a chapter—and a healthy one looked at in proper perspective—in the history of the cordial relations that have prevailed between the TTOA and Texaco. Although to some this slight change in the transportation clause was a small matter for which to turn down substantial gains, with the risk that in any subsequent meetings these gains could not be dated back to the time originally agreed upon, there was a matter of pride and position involved. Texaco bargains with the National Maritime Union for its unlicensed personnel, and in their agreements all transportation is first class. While it is true unlicensed personnel do not receive transportation when going on and returning from vacation as is provided in the officers' agreement, in the rare cases in which they are entitled to transportation it is first class. And since the transportation Texaco officers previously received had been first class, the change to economy class was difficult to accept. Frequent mention was made by individual officers in their criticism of the agreement of occasions when they would be flying on the same plane with an unlicensed crew member. The seaman would be flying first class at company expense; the officer under the terms of the agreement—which had been rejected—would be required to fly economy class. The issue was more emotional than economic. Both parties finally recognized this. When the renegotiated Memorandum of Understanding was submitted to the membership it was approved by a substantial majority—167 in favor, 32 against.[14]

NOTES

1. JSTOA, *Official Records,* 1967.
2. Masters, Mates and Pilots, ILA/AFL–CIO, *Master Collective Bargaining Agreement,* June 16, 1972, New York.
3. JSTOA, *News Letter,* May 14, 1968.
4. Certification of Results, JSTOA Constitutional Amendment Ballot, June 5, 1968.
5. JSTOA, *News Letter,* March 25, 1968.
6. Memorandum of Understanding, JSTOA and Marine Department, Humble Oil and Refining Company, December 19, 1968.
7. JSTOA, *News Letter,* January 8, 1969.
8. Certification of Results, Ratification ballot, American Arbitration Association, February 17, 1969.
9. *Ibid.*
10. TTOA, *News Letter,* November 22, 1969.
11. TTOA, *Official Records,* December 22, 1969.
12. TTOA, *News Letter,* January 26, 1970.
13. *Ibid.*
14. TTOA, *Official Records,* March 2, 1973.

7

Comparing the Economic Package

MEANWHILE IN MOBIL the 20-year, no-age pension plan finally had been negotiated. To reach agreement, however, it had been necessary to trade off participation in the company-wide benefit plans, including the savings plan, for a new set of benefit plans which were not nearly as attractive. After the pension hurdle had been overcome negotiations for wage increases and other improvements proceeded smoothly in the years 1968 and 1969. Although the Mobil association was aware that in Exxon, Texaco, and Getty the pensions were better because they had not been forced to forgo the company career-type pension to secure the special seagoing 20-year pension, no immediate effort was made by the Mobil independent to modify their agreement in this area.

An interesting development in the 1968 Mobil negotiations involved the wage pattern. The agreement reached resulted in moving Mobil's starting wage to the highest plateau in the industry. This became important later when national unions negotiated an overtime formula of straight time, time-and-one-quarter, and time-and-one-half, programed over a three-year period. The higher base-wage rate in Mobil meant that, if they followed this overtime formula (and they did), after the third year of a three-year agreement when time-and-one-half became the rate, Mobil's overtime rate would be distinctly higher than that paid elsewhere. This happened.

In the 1972 negotiations the company therefore sought to correct this situation by not offering any increase in the overtime rate—although approximately 6 percent increases had been negotiated by national unions and by the independent TTOA in both wages and overtime.

Returning to the 1968 negotiations: the starting wage effective January 1, 1969, and the amount of increase which this new wage represented over the previous wage negotiated by the MTOA were as follows:[1]

TABLE IX

	New Starting Wage	Amount of Increase Per Month
Master	$1,801	$115
Chief Engineer	1,746	115
CM–1AE	1,175	75
2M–2AE	1,025	65
3M–3AE	938	60

In the fall of 1969 for the first time since the National Maritime Union 1939 tanker strike, Mobil ships were struck. The strike was called by the union representing the unlicensed personnel, OCAW (AFL–CIO) Maritime Local 880. This union, previously known as the Socony Vacuum Tanker Mens Association, had originated as a result of the 1939 tanker strike. It remained independent until it affiliated with the Oil, Chemical and Atomic Workers International Union (AFL–CIO) in 1968.

Negotiations with the company, after this affiliation, were masterminded by the shore-based OCAW whose decisions generally were made at their Denver, Colorado headquarters. The strike was not primarily over money, but rather to have the seagoing agreement terminate at the same time that all agreements negotiated by the OCAW terminated, namely, December 31. The purpose was to give the OCAW greater bargaining leverage and strike strength should an impasse occur in their bargaining with those major oil companies whose employees were represented by them. If they could effectively slow down or immobilize the company's vessels at the same time they shut down the Mobil refinery (whose employees they represented), they would be able to hurt the company more than if Mobil could move their vessels at will, obtaining cargoes in various places and delivering them to areas where there were no work stoppages. It was this flexibility to operate that the OCAW were seeking to negate. The strike lasted 61 days. The OCAW did not achieve their objective.

During this period the officers represented by the MTOA remained aboard the vessels to keep them in readiness whenever the strike terminated. There was a contract in effect between the MTOA and the company, and the association's executive committee did not feel that it should or could do anything but honor that contract. The company did the same. The association informed the company that the officers would do whatever work was required under their contract as officers—but only as officers. The company accepted this position and emphasized that no officer would be used to do work other than that normally done by an officer. The officers remained on pay and received all the benefits provided under the terms of the agreement, including earned vacation (paid leave). During the period of the strike, the association was readying its proposals for the next round of negotiations scheduled to begin in December of that year.

1969 was the year in which the largest money-gains ever negotiated at a single sitting in the maritime industry were bargained by national and independent unions. Generally the agreements were for a three-year period. The value of the increases in wages and overtime over the three-year period amounted to 40 per cent of 1969 income. The reason why these money gains were so substantial resulted from a formula which provided that overtime in excess of 8 hours in any one day or in excess of 40 hours in any one week was to be paid for in the first year of a three-year contract at the straight-time rate, in the second year at time-and-one-quarter, and in the third year at time-and-one-half of the base rate. Straight time was determined by dividing 173.3 (the equivalent of 40 hours per week for a 30-day period) into the regular monthly base pay.

For those not familiar with the wage and overtime pattern in the maritime industry, overtime had been payable not just for work in excess of 8 hours, but for work many times within the 8-hour spread. Sometimes this was termed penalty pay, premium pay, or tank-cleaning money. Because these payments were for work not in excess of 8 hours, and further because the maritime industry had been exempt from the Wages and Hours Act which provided that shoreside employees be paid at the rate of time-and-one-half for work in excess of 40 hours in one week, fixed overtime rates on a negotiated basis had been the rule in the maritime industry for many years, with the overtime rate bearing little resemblance to straight-time hourly rates. This concept changed in 1969.

The result of the bargaining in Mobil, which probably is the best example of how this new formula worked out in practice, provided for a 6 percent increase in the starting wage for all officers for each of the three years—namely, the years beginning January 1, 1970, January 1, 1971, and January 1, 1972. The overtime-rate formula became straight time during the first year, time-and-one-quarter during the second year, and time-and-one-half during the third year. Saturdays, Sundays, and holidays at sea or in port previously had been designated overtime days. The overtime rate that had been payable in the 1969 agreement for a chief mate or first assistant engineer in Mobil was $4.58 per hour. This was payable to watchstanding officers every Saturday and Sunday at sea or in port, as well as for holidays. This overtime was in addition to the regular wage for these days. Overtime also was paid for work performed or watches stood in excess of 8 hours in any day.

Under the agreement that was to begin January 1, 1970, the overtime rate for a chief mate or first assistant engineer jumped from $4.58 to $7.19 per hour. On January 1, 1971, it became $9.53 per hour, and on January 1, 1972, it rose to $12.12 per hour. So that in the short period from January 1, 1969, to January 1, 1972, the overtime rate had almost tripled. The reason for this was, first the wages themselves increased 6 per cent in each of the three years, and second, the formula for the payment of overtime (namely, straight time, time-and-one-quarter, and finally time-and-one-half) on the higher base wage had a compounding effect.[2]

As a result of the sharply increased overtime rate for mates and assistant engineers, and the fact that they earned overtime for every Saturday and Sunday whether the vessel was at sea or in port, the total compensation of these officers could be expected to exceed that of the master and chief engineer. To prevent this, a monthly cash allowance payable the full 12 months (overtime was payable to mates and assistant engineers only when assigned to a vessel—8 months in the year) was added to the base pay of the master and chief engineer. In the first year of the contract the cash allowance was $450 per month for the master and $425 per month for the chief engineer. In the second year the master received $550 per month and the chief engineer $525. In the third year these amounts became $650 per month for the master and $625 for the chief engineer. Fortunately for the officers these increases in wages, overtime rates, and the cash allowances had been negotiated well before President Nixon's wage-freeze announcement. Because of this they were allowed to be paid even though they exceeded the wage guidelines in the last year of the three-year agreement.

In the 1972 negotiations for an agreement to begin January 1, 1973, Mobil was quick to remind the association that the money gains in the past three years had been "astronomical" (company language), and as far as the overtime rates were concerned, because of the higher base wage in Mobil, their overtime rate, the company argued, had become uncompetitive with the rest of the industry. For example, the national unions with a lower base wage, under the new overtime formula of time-and-one-half in the third year, also would have a lower overtime rate than Mobil. The overtime rate for a chief mate and first assistant engineer under the national-union contract in the third year of their contract became $10.77; whereas in the third year of Mobil's contract the overtime rate became $12.12 per hour. And this was paid automatically for a *minimum* of 70 hours per month. These 70 hours represented Saturdays, Sundays, and holidays at sea or in port.

Despite these substantial improvements in wages and overtime there still was some grumbling, especially among the masters and chief engineers who, even with the cash allowance payable on top of their new base wages and payable 12 months a year, claimed (and correctly) that in many instances a first assistant's or a chief mate's earnings topped theirs—at least while they both were on the same vessel. The company tried to counter this complaint by pointing out that the cash allowance was payable annually, which included the time the master and chief engineer were on paid leave (4 months a year vacation); whereas overtime was payable to the other officers only while assigned to a vessel (8 months a year). But the grumbling continued.

Mates and assistant engineers also received overtime for all work performed or watches stood in excess of 8 hours per day. This is variable. It never is easy to determine what is equitable in the distribution of monies paid for both work *and* responsibility, especially where overtime is paid to some and not to others. Watchstanding officers are working supervisors. (Overtime was not paid to masters and chief engineers whose responsibility was a 24-hour-a-day one.) A further contributing fact to the unevenness of the money distribution is the pattern of work for which overtime is paid.

On some ships there is a considerable amount of work to do either because ship repairs are constant or because of the nature of the ship's trade—including the carrying of multiple grades of cargo. These circumstances resulted in increased income for those required to perform this work. In these instances the chief mate and first assistant are the ones upon whom the bulk of this burden falls and who, of course, benefit in their earnings. These additional earnings could result, and have resulted, in the chief mate's "paying off" at the end of a voyage with more money than the master. Therefore, despite the size of the increases in their total compensation (wages and cash allowances), the masters and chief engineers were not completely happy because they did not feel, regardless of conditions, that a subordinate officer should have greater earnings on the same ship than the senior officers.

The attractiveness of the base wage and overtime rates negotiated in Mobil vis-à-vis national unions and other independent unions did not constitute the whole picture as far as earnings and other conditions of employment are concerned. The Mobil officer was not necessarily ahead of his counterpart in the industry in total take-home pay. Each agreement must be examined in its entirety, especially as to how it affects the individuals working under it. It would be simplistic to say that the Mobil agreement was a better agreement than either the national-union agreements or the agreements negotiated by other independent unions. The problem lies in the difficulty in making comparisons.

In the national unions for example there is a manning scale which represents a considerable cost to the company by virtue of the required addition of two officers. In the past where the two officers could not be supplied, their wages were divided among the remaining officers on the ship (now these monies revert to the union). On the other hand, there is some loss in overtime income for the individual officer when additional officers are carried, since there are more of them to share the workload.

There are other areas in national-union agreements where payments are made that in similar circumstances may not be made by the terms of the independent-union agreements. Independent unions, however, over the years have negotiated substantial payments for "length of service." This is not done by national unions since their structure and operation almost precludes continuous employment with one company. In addition licensed officers represented by independent unions receive other direct monetary and fringe benefits not available to those working under national-union agreements. Sick-leave pay is just one of these.

To indicate how misleading certain base-wage comparisons can be, the following example is cited. The 1973 negotiations between American Trading Transportation Company (a tanker company but not an oil company) and the independent union representing their deck and engine officers, the American Tanker Officers Association, resulted in a higher base wage than that negotiated by national unions in June of 1972 and higher in general than that negotiated by independent unions representing licensed officers in the major oil companies in late 1972 and early 1973. The following figures indicate these differences.

TABLE X
MONTHLY BASE WAGES
(INCLUDING SUPPLEMENTS FOR MASTERS)

	Masters, Mates & Pilots (AFL–CIO)[3]	Mobil (Ind.)[4]	Texaco (Ind.)[5]	ATOA (Ind.)[6]
Master	$2,662.07	$2,999.02	$2,971	$3,057
Chief Officer	1,314.91	1,483.44	1,415	2,097
Second Officer	1,162.76	1,293.79	1,256	1,818
Third Officer	1,010.60	1,184.18	1,134	1,648

The above figures, however, do not and cannot tell the full story because the philosophy of American Trading Transportation Company and the union with which they bargain is to put as much into the base wage as possible. Overtime *as such* is not paid for Saturdays and Sundays as is true in the rest of the industry. In American Trading it is buried in the base pay. Overtime is payable for work only in excess of 8 hours in any one day. Clearly there is considerable difficulty in interpreting these differences in the compensation structure. Unless one is thoroughly familiar both with the industry and with the desires of the particular bargaining groups as to what they believe is in their best interests, one cannot readily make a value judgment in regard to one agreement vis-à-vis any other agreement, except as a total package, including guaranteed annual employment.

Apart from differences in base wages among the various maritime groups representing licensed officers, there are differences in overtime monies earned by officers under the terms of agreements negotiated by the several independent unions. A case in point involves the agreement negotiated in 1972 by the TTOA which provided greater annual compensation than the 1973 Mobil agreement for the chief mate and first assistant engineer in a particular area despite the difference in overtime rates. Unquestionably the $10.75 per hour regular overtime rate at which a chief mate in Texaco was paid was considerably less than the $12.12 rate payable under the Mobil agreement. However, Texaco had a clause in their agreement which provided that when a ship is in port weekdays between 5 P.M. and 8 A.M., whether cargo is being worked or not, payment at the regular overtime rate ($10.75 per hour for the chief mate) instead of at the penalty rate be paid for *all such work*.[7] The penalty rate of $4.23 per hour was payable for such work in port in Mobil, as well as elsewhere in the industry at that time, including the national unions.

Vessels are in port, at least in the Texaco situation, approximately 10 days per month. Of these 10 days, 7 days are week days (when such overtime is payable between 5 P.M. and 8 A.M.). In the case of the chief mate, 7 of his 8 hours of work each day are overtime hours—because his regular hours of watch are 4 to 8 (from 5 P.M. to 8 P.M. and from 4 A.M. to 8 A.M. total 7 overtime hours). These hours at the regular overtime rate, as worked out on the blackboard during the Texaco negotiations, indicated that a Texaco chief mate or first assistant engineer would earn $4,300 for the 8 months of the year during which he was on the ship (the other 4 months are his paid-leave time) *just for port time*. (Texaco officers, however, received port relief. When this occurred, port overtime would not be payable.) Under national union contracts in 1971 and under the Mobil contract, the same number of hours payable at the penalty rate of $4.23 per hour totalled $1,692 for the year for the chief mate and first assistant engineer. The difference for this item alone was substantial.

In the Getty Oil Company's American-flag fleet licensed officers (deck and engine) and unlicensed seamen have been represented by independent unions since before World War II. Both were certified by the National Labor Relations Board following their victories over national unions. Each has bargained successfully for more than thirty years, bringing the employees they represent constantly improved wages and working conditions and achieving this without interrupting the company's continuity of operation; and without loss of wages to the employees.

The formula for this joint success is similar to that of other independent unions. Employees themselves elect representatives who possess a special strength—their intimate knowledge of what the employees they represent really want, and an intuitive sense of what can be achieved by a logical and determined presentation of these wants. This, plus an understanding management which recognizes that the opportunity to deal directly with their employees by local-level bargaining is a labor-relations luxury, has insured success. By negotiating agreements that provide at least the prevailing wage in the industry; by making a serious effort to treat their employees as an integral part of the Getty group; and by being eminently fair in its dealings with the Getty Tanker

Men's Association (GTMA) and the Getty Tanker Officers Association (GTOA), the company's marine management has indicated that it is fully aware of this luxury.

Bargaining collectively is a continuing process. It is not like a transaction in which after it has been once consummated the parties never meet again. In bargaining collectively it can be presumed that essentially the same people will be face to face next year and the year after that. This knowledge, plus the built-in advantage of bargaining on the local level for both parties, has contributed to the success these small organizations may claim as theirs over the years. But words alone are not proof of that success. Rather the terms of the contracts negotiated by them form the proof. Especially when the contracts are laid side by side contracts in the same industry covering similar employees can that success be spelled out in dollars and cents. The contract comparison below is among five organizations representing unlicensed seamen on East Coast deep-sea tankers. Two of these organizations are independent unions—GTMA and Esso Seamen's Association (ESA); one is the National Maritime Union (AFL–CIO) which represents the bulk of unlicensed seamen on the East Coast; one is the Seafarers International Union (AFL–CIO) which represents seamen in several East Coast shipping companies; and one is Maritime Local 880 of the OCAW (AFL–CIO) which represents Mobil seamen.

The comparison is confined to base wages for typical ratings negotiated in 1973 by three of these organizations and in 1972 by the other two. It is clear that in base wages alone for these representative ratings the GTMA is out in front. (TABLE XI)

True, overtime rates and the circumstances under which overtime is earned are not included, but those familiar with the industry know that generally the differences, especially as far as rates are concerned, are minimal. Vacations, excepting the Exxon group (ESA) who have been on a "15 for 30" basis for more than ten years, are almost identical—14 for 30.

However, there are several important differences between the independent union groups (GTMA and ESA) and the national union groups (NMU and SIU). Both the GTMA and the ESA have negotiated additional compensation for length of service. By the terms of the GTMA agreement this additional remuneration begins after one year of service and increases after two, three, five, seven and one-half, and ten years of company service. The amounts range from $14 per month to $67 per month for an

TABLE XI

	1972 ESA[8]	1972 OCAW[9]	1973 NMU[10]	1973 SIU[11]	1973 GTMA[12]
Boatswain	*	$740.61	$816.49	$817.54	$834
Able Seaman	585	568.59	589.47	590.52	630
Ordinary Seaman	468	446.28	467.21	468.26	491
Pumpman	800	770.43	823.97	825.02	866
Oiler	585	568.59	589.47	590.52	622
Wiper	*	505.60	541.14	542.19	568
Steward	†	798.84	819.75	820.80	917‡
Second Cook	608	590.20	613.23	614.28	684
Messman	450	446.28	451.62	452.67	479

* Not carried
† Represented by Exxon Stewards Organization
‡ Steward-cook

A.B. (able-bodied seaman, the most frequently used rating when discussing wage rates and other compensation for unlicensed personnel). In addition to these specific dollar differences based on length of service, fringe benefits, such as pensions, life insurance, sick pay, and savings-plan contributions by the company, are increased automatically with any increase in base pay. Under national-union agreements fringe benefits are predicated on the amount per-day, per-man paid into the union fund. The determination as to what the benefits shall be and who is eligible for them is made by the union. A further plus for a Getty seaman is the fact that once he secures a job with Getty he can be reasonably assured he will be able to continue in it as long as his work is satisfactory and he wishes to remain. He is a Getty employee and is treated as such. Under the shipping rules of national unions, depending upon his type of book membership, a seaman's period of employment may vary. Time between ships (during which he is off pay) is generally spent at the union shipping hall or close to it. He does not identify with a particular employer. He identifies with the union for both employment opportunities and fringe benefits, including earned vacation.

These few examples are furnished to indicate that negotiations as carried on by independent unions are just as vigorous and at least as productive (if the yardstick is annual earnings including fringes) as those carried on by national unions. Though there are differences, and arguments from contracts negotiated elsewhere are used by both management and the bargaining teams of the independents (to favor their respective position), whatever agreement finally is reached presumably is satisfactory, since membership approval is necessary. And there are the added benefits—namely, employees are never off pay, and the operation of the company's vessels is never interrupted. These spill over to the general public in the labor stability they represent.

NOTES

1. Agreement, between Mobil Oil Corporation, Marine Transportation Department, Gulf–East Coast Fleet and MTOA (Ind.), January 1, 1969.
2. Agreement, between Mobil Oil Corporation, Marine Transportation Department, Gulf–East Coast Fleet and MTOA (Ind.), January 1, 1970.
3. Agreement, Masters, Mates and Pilots (AFL–CIO) and East Coast Tanker Companies, June 16, 1972.
4. Agreement, between Mobil Oil Corporation, Marine Transportation Department, Gulf–East Coast Fleet and MTOA (Ind.), January 1, 1973.
5. Agreement, between Texaco Inc., Marine Department, and TTOA, September 1, 1973.
6. Agreement, between American Trading Transportation Co., Inc. and American Tanker Officers Association, February 1, 1973.
7. Agreement, between Texaco, Inc., Marine Department, and TTOA, September 1, 1971.
8. Amendment to Agreement, Exxon Company, U.S.A. (a division of Exxon Corporation), Marine Department, successor by merger to Humble Oil and Refining Company, and Esso Seamen's Association, March 5, 1971, amended effective September 1, 1972.
9. Agreement, OCAW (AFL–CIO), Maritime Local 880 and Mobil Oil Company, August 1, 1972.
10. Agreement, National Maritime Union (AFL–CIO) and East Coast Tanker Companies, June 16, 1972.
11. Memorandum of Understanding, Seafarers International Union of North America, Atlantic, Gulf, Lakes and Inland Waters District (AFL–CIO), June 16, 1972.
12. Addendum to Agreement, Getty Oil Company (Eastern Operations) Inc., Supply and Distribution Department–Marine Section, and GTMA (Ind.), effective March 1, 1973.

8

Settling Grievances

THE BARGAINING PROCESS does not stop with the signing of a contract. It is only the beginning. The implementation of contracts, vows, understandings, and the like, becomes the lifeblood coursing through the arteries of all institutional arrangements and structures in society.

The fulfilling of a contract entered into between the employer and the union constitutes the administration of that instrument. This includes not merely the payment of the wages and overtime, plus providing the working conditions agreed to by both parties, but clarifications and interpretations of the contract; and where necessary, the arbitration of disputes that almost inevitably arise under it. No matter how zealously the parties work to conclude an agreement, it is not always easy to write its terms clearly and precisely. At some later date when a determination must be made as to what a particular part of an agreement means, and the parties cannot agree on the interpretation, they must either agree to accept the interpretation of one of the parties, or take the matter to arbitration.

While there is no substitute for genuine good faith, even where this does prevail there can be honest differences of opinion as to meanings of clauses in contracts. If the parties have a reasonably cordial relationship—which normally can be expected to exist where local-level bargaining exists—one party or the other may on occasion graciously accept an adverse interpretation. This is somewhat risky, but if the interpretation is limited to the one case and no precedents are apt to result no great harm is done. As a matter of fact good could result. Meanwhile, the mortar for making the agreement become a firmer foundation for respectful relations between the parties is being applied—and that is important. Too many times agreements, once made, languish on the vine, simply because they have not played their proper role in that continuing dialogue called human relations.

Some managements consider this moribund situation to be a plus. No grievances, they say, equal employee happiness. No one should suggest that grievances be dredged up just for their irritant value. This would constitute creeping chaos and would occur only to individuals who require psychiatric attention. But the very nature of man, the myriad situations that he faces daily, and the decisions he must make in respect to these situations, his interpersonal relations with his fellow employees, plus the necessity to maintain a proper flow of communications between himself and his supervisors, are bound to unsettle the equilibrium a negotiated contract seeks to provide.

The following case will illustrate the difficulty that can develop in seeking to carry out the provisions of an agreement. A clause in the JSTOA agreement read "no unnecessary work shall be performed on Saturdays, Sundays, or any of the holidays in Article VI of this agreement or between the hours of 5:00 P.M. and 8:00 A.M." [1] But to define "unnecessary" in some circumstances would tax the wisdom of a Solomon. Past practice helps to define it and there are clear-cut situations where work on Saturday or Sunday is *necessary*—securing a ship when the weather suddenly changes and the vessel is in danger of becoming unmoored, or where there is a breakdown at sea and all engineers are required to bear a hand with the repairs. There are equally clear cases where the work is routine, and common sense plus past practice dictate it as unnecessary to be performed on Saturday or Sunday.

But there are borderline cases when the judgment of a supervisor becomes, at least for the moment, the determining factor. Such a situation occurred aboard the *Esso Miami* on Sunday, February 7, 1971. This vessel carried a "day working" chief mate and a "day working" first assistant engineer in addition to the three watchstanding officers in each of the two departments—deck and engine. Normally these day-working officers worked only on weekdays. However, when there was necessary work to be done on Saturday or Sunday in accordance with the language of the contract, it was done. On Sunday February 7 the chief engineer ordered the first assistant engineer to perform work that the first assistant felt was unnecessary. In the opinion of the first assistant the work ordered by the chief—removing the lagging from the six-inch main steam line which was leaking—could have waited until Monday. His belief, based on his years of experience as an engineer, was that the leak was such as to require that it be repaired in a shipyard. Therefore the work of removing the lagging on Sunday was not necessary since, without danger to the ship, it could wait until Monday. Because friction had developed between these two officers previously, their ability to communicate had been impaired. It was not made clear by the chief engineer to the first assistant that, in the chief engineer's opinion, the work was *necessary*. Because the company supported the chief engineer the case finally was adjudicated via arbitration, in accordance with the terms of the agreement relating to unresolved grievances. This was expensive but in this instance, at least, there was no other way.

At the arbitration hearing, according to the testimony of the first assistant engineer, the chief had told him, "on this ship you work seven days a week." No attempt apparently had been made to indicate to the first assistant engineer that, in the judgment of the chief engineer, the work in question was necessary. Maurice S. Trotta, an experienced arbitrator and professor of labor relations at New York University, stated in his opinion:

> The company is justified in arguing that it is almost impossible to set standards as to what is "necessary work" because too many factors are involved. The chief engineer's opinion should be followed. If the union feels that the work being assigned by him is not in fact necessary, a grievance may be filed.
>
> To avoid problems, the chief engineer should clearly state that he believes the work is necessary. If Chief Leavins had done so in the instant case and not depended on unspoken assumptions, this case might not have arisen. Even if we hold that work on the evaporator and the six-inch main line was necessary, we are still faced with the primary cause of this grievance, which is whether the chief engineer properly interpreted the contract. I find that by his words and attitudes the chief engineer gave Mr. Rose a legitimate reason for filing a grievance on the grounds that he was misinterpreting the contract.
>
> He gave Mr. Rose reason to believe that he would be required to perform on Saturdays, Sundays and holidays whatever work was available and needed to be done irrespective of whether it was "necessary" or "unnecessary." The company freely admits that the contract provides that unnecessary work need not be performed on Saturdays, Sundays and holidays.[2]

After stating his opinion, Professor Trotta made the following award:

> The chief engineer by his attitude and words gave the grievant reason to believe that contrary to the provisions of the contract he

would be required to perform on Saturdays, Sundays and holidays, whatever work was available and needed to be done irrespective of whether it was necessary or unnecessary.[3]

This represented a victory for the association. Money was not involved, but the inviolability of the contract was. It could be argued, as did the arbitrator, that the situation never should have arisen; but this is a little like saying that everyone *always* should agree; that lines of communication *always* should be open; and that understandings and instructions *always* should be clear. Obviously this ideal never should be neglected; however, in this instance the arbitrator held that it had been. As a result of this arbitration there was a better understanding of what constituted "necessary" and "unnecessary" work, and, more importantly, improved communications, especially between chief engineers and their assistants. The company indicated its displeasure that the association had gone to arbitration on the matter. But there were times when the association felt the company allowed their top supervisors too much leeway. This was one of them. Arbitration may not be the most desirable method to resolve differences that arise between parties to a labor agreement. However, this approach is preferable to wildcat strikes, sit-downs, and slow-downs so frequently permitted or authorized by national unions.

In December 1969 a case involving the volatile issue of oil pollution occurred on a Humble Oil (Exxon) ship. The chief mate of the vessel was judged responsible for a small "spill" and given a 14-day suspension by the company. Taken up by the JSTOA at the request of the aggrieved officer, it became a two-year battle between the JSTOA and the company before the matter was resolved. The case highlights the delicate line of demarcation between management's right to manage and a legitimate questioning of a decision made by management which resulted in disciplinary measures against the individual employee.

No one is more desirous of being considered a "good citizen" in the broadest sense of that term than a major oil company. Frequently targets for criticism because of their alleged power to manipulate things and people to their own advantage, major oil companies work zealously to confine this criticism to those cases where they may have been in error. These efforts are not advertising gimmicks or Madison Avenue "soft sell" approaches to mesmerize the public or paint something gray that is black.

Responsible corporations like responsible citizens everywhere are concerned when charges of irresponsibility, wild or otherwise, are made. This author has observed the most costly and circumspect conduct by major oil companies in the current nationwide concern—oil pollution. Nowhere perhaps can this concern for prevention of pollution be witnessed better than in the attention that is paid to preventing possible spills and other accidents that could, and do, result in polluting rivers, bays, and shorelines.*

There is such emphasis on the prevention of pollution at sea or in port by the officialdom of major oil companies that ships' officers consider it "top management phobia." And it has added to the anxiety and tension especially among deck officers who supervise the loading and discharge of hundreds of thousands of barrels of cargo each voyage. In the 1972 bargaining sessions between the TTOA and Texaco, the subject of the status of licensed officers involved in oil pollution, where no negligence existed, consumed many hours of discussion and heated debate as to what protection an innocent officer in a pollution-resulting accident might be assured of from the company. At the conclusion of the meetings the association was satisfied that the company would provide the officers with whatever legal assistance might be necessary. This would be in the interest of both the officer and the company since the officer is the agent of the company.[4]

Pollution prevention clearly has top priority in the petroleum industry. Managements are concerned about the overreaction of environmentalists and others to the spilling of a "cupful of oil." They issue countless "dos" and "don'ts" to personnel on ships which they own or control. And they scrupulously monitor their implementation. Apart from the company's concern, a licensed officer's pride in his work suffers if he becomes involved in a spill or pollution. So when two barrels of Ketone (a rapidly evaporating solvent) were flushed on the deck of the *Esso Florence* on October 18, 1969 at the dock in Bayway, New Jersey, and the Coast Guard spotted some of it leaking from two of the ship's scuppers into the Kill Van Kull, the chief mate was in deep trouble.

To the layman, at first glance, flushing any kind of petroleum cargo on deck seems incomprehensible, and the ultimate in indifference to the environment. But like many things that circum-

---

* In Exxon retired seagoing officers are employed on a per diem basis to board company vessels, both American- and foreign-flag, to be certain that everything possible is done to prevent a spill in the loading and discharging of cargos.

stantially are incriminating, the chief mate in the instant case had an explanation that made sense. The deck itself with the scuppers in place is a "contained" area, and this particular cargo—Ketone—disappears quickly via evaporation. On October 19, the day following the spill, he prepared his account of what happened to enable the master of the vessel to make a full report of the incident to the company at Houston.

> Dear Sir:
> On October 18, 1969, in preparation for discharge of Ketone feed it was decided to flush approximately two barrels of Ketone on deck until the chemist passed the cargo as clear and free of chlorides. The deck scuppers were in place and preparations were made to scoop up the Ketone and put it in slop drums. This decision being made inasmuch as there is no arrangement whereby the Ketone could be flushed on the dock. (That is what the dock claims.)
> At 16:30 the U. S. Coast Guard inspection party came down the dock and noticed that two scupper plugs were leaking. Many pictures were taken and much running about by U. S. Coast Guard personnel. The crew replaced the faulty scupper plugs and the excess remaining on the deck was put into slop buckets.
> I would judge that at the most, the cargo that leaked into the Kills was less than one barrel. The Ketone as it hit the water turns the water creamy and it looks worse than it really is. However, the leak was there.
> This flushing on deck is usual routine as it is usually impossible to flush into a cargo tank. The cargo we had in the nearby tanks was not compatible, thereby eliminating the possibility of flushing into these tanks. The amount of cargo picked up from the deck did not fill a thirty gallon slop can.
> I trust that the information above will be sufficient to fully explain the incident.[5]

In his report dated October 21 to the Port Captain at Houston, the master of the *Esso Florence* stated:

> About 12:30 Mr. Parker came to me and reported that he had flushed some Ketone on deck to clean the line and some of it had seeped over the side through the scupper plugs, and that the Coast Guard boarding party was aboard making a record of the incident. Needless to say I was shocked over this revelation and told Mr. Parker that he should not have flushed the product on deck under any circumstances regardless of what the chemist wanted.
> It was most unfortunate and embarrassing that the chief mate took upon himself to flush the line on deck rather than consult

the night supervisor to find some means of displacing the line ashore in view of the stringent rules imposed by the Coast Guard. Furthermore, the scupper plugs should have been checked for leakage before any form of cargo operation was commenced.

The Coast Guard took statements from both the chief mate and second mate (who was on watch at the time) and claimed violation of Article 46 CFR 35,3510 (closing of scupper and sea valves).[6]

On October 31 a company investigating committee met to review the case. The chief mate was not present at the investigation, nor was there an opportunity given the JSTOA to testify on his behalf. The conclusion reached by the company investigating committee was that the chief mate had

> exercised poor judgment in that . . .
> 1. He should have flushed the Ketone line at sea.
> 2. He should have made sure that the scupper plugs were properly installed.
> 3. Since he decided to flush the line at the dock, he should have used drums or slop cans.
>
> Considering that Captain Johnson had called Mr. Parker's attention to Circular Letter M-799 immediately prior to flushing of the line, Mr. Parker's subsequent action indicates a complete disregard of required and necessary precautions.[7]

The company committee reported their findings to the general manager of the Marine Department on November 10 and recommended that "Mr. Parker be suspended without pay for 14 days and reprimanded in writing, including a warning that any similar lapses on his part will result in severe disciplinary measures." The company noted that Mr. Parker was first employed in 1947 and had served as a licensed officer continuously and that "most recent progress reports are above average."[8]

On December 2 the operations manager, by letter, informed the chief mate of his suspension.[9] In that letter stress was placed on the company's effort to apprise all masters and chief mates of the seriousness of pollution by citing the company's Circular Letter M-799 which emphasized the obligation on all officers to comply with Tank Vessel Regulations issued by the Coast Guard to reduce or eliminate the possibility of pollution.

> Captain T. A. Johnson advises that, while the ship was in the Kills enroute to Bayway, you were given a copy of Circular Letter M-799, which deals with observance of Coast Guard regulations,

and specifically cautioned as to its contents. In spite of the warning regarding improper plugging of scuppers, you elected to pump Ketone on deck without assurance that the scupper plugs were tight, thus indicating complete disregard of certain Coast Guard regulations as well as our attempt to assist you in the observance of such.

The chief mate received the letter dated December 2 from the operations manager on December 11 at Salem, Massachusetts. His first reaction was one of shock and disbelief; as he indicated in his sharply worded reply to the operations manager—

> Your communication of December 2, 1969, was received after docking at Salem, Massachusetts, on December 11, 1969.
>
> Having spent the previous 24 hours on the bridge due to reduced visibility, then fog; and after clearing of fog, navigating in restricted waters due to fishing fleets and final approach to port, climaxing with docking of the vessel at Salem, I'll assure you that your communication was received as an extremely foul blow. However, I managed to "maintain my cool," and restrained myself from sending off a reply until I felt myself fully rested from extra long hours on the bridge. This action on my part has made it possible for me to recall somewhat more clearly the happenings leading up to, during, and after the incident aboard the ss "Esso Florence."
>
> In regard to Circular Letter M-799, the first time I was made aware of its presence was when I returned to my room on the "Esso Florence" *after* the incident, and saw the letter laying on my desk. So far as I can recall, this letter was not given to me by Capt. T. A. Johnson, and contrary to anything he has said, he DID NOT (I repeat, he DID NOT) make its presence known to me, nor did he caution me as to its contents. If he has said otherwise, I feel that he has become extremely careless in the handling of the truth.
>
> Even had Capt. T. A. Johnson made its presence and contents known to me, I shall assure you that the routine I use in preparation for discharge of cargo does indeed include proper distribution of slop buckets at risers; tightness of all scuppers; tightness of sea-cocks, overboard and skin valves on stripper systems. There is nothing overlooked in my routine before arrival at the discharge dock and prior to discharge of cargo. How else do you think that I have been able to maintain what I believe to be a perfect record since the start of my employment with Humble Oil and Refining Company, Marine Division, and predecessor marine affiliates on August 16, 1947? It is this record that you have seen fit to damage by your suspension of me for 14 days without a formal hearing.[10]

He followed this letter with one a few days later to the general manager asking to meet with him "to discuss the details of the incident for which management has seen fit to suspend me for 14 days." [11] But the general manager suffered a fatal heart attack on December 24. Meanwhile Mr. Parker brought the matter to the attention of the association which had been meeting with management to negotiate a new agreement. The company was adamant in refusing to reverse their decision. Part of their refusal was in the form of a rebuttal to the association's charge that the grievance procedure in the contract had been violated in that Mr. Parker had had no opportunity to enlist the aid of the association. On October 29, 1970 the company wrote the association:

> ... This confirms our advice at our meeting of October 20, that the facts concerning the suspension of Mr. Parker have been reviewed at the third step of the grievance procedure. We find no violation of the contract. The alleged grievance is denied.[12]

The association still persisted, however, in its belief that Mr. Parker had not had an opportunity fully to present his case. Therefore on June 9, 1971 the association notified the company that it was prepared to take the case to arbitration.

> Dear Sirs:
> This will refer to your letter dated October 29, 1970, regarding the above member of this association. This matter has been discussed with you since that time, but at the moment without success, at least as far as changing the disciplinary action taken by the company.
> Normally we would be proceeding to the 4th Step but we are of the opinion that this 4th Step has already been taken via meetings between the association and the company in respect to the above. Therefore, we are hereby notifying the company that we are about to proceed to arbitration under Article XI of the Agreement.
> The question to be arbitrated, in our opinion, is—Did the company act arbitrarily in suspending Charles Parker for fourteen days without a formal hearing for alleged negligence regarding the scupper plugs aboard the s.s. "Esso Florence" when the vessel was discharging its cargo at Bayway, New Jersey, on or about the beginning of December, 1969?
>
> Very truly yours,
> JERSEY STANDARD TANKER OFFICERS ASSOCIATION[13]

On August 9, 1971, the assistant general manager wrote a conciliatory letter to the association. He took note that despite the company's position at a meeting with the association's executive committee on June 20, 1970, where they reaffirmed their disciplinary decision, the company now was willing to meet with the association, and have Mr. Parker present to give his side of the story and answer questions. . . .

> Your letter of June 9, 1971 raised the question of whether Captain Parker [normal promotion routine in the meantime had resulted in Parker's promotion to captain] was afforded the opportunity of a formal hearing prior to his suspension. The Accident Investigation Committee on October 31, 1969 reviewed the available facts concerning the incident in question, and recommended disciplinary action. Captain Parker, according to the records, did not appear before the committee, but his report to the ship's Master was part of the information available to the committee. However, a thorough review of our records on this case, prompted by your June 9, 1971 letter, together with recent discussions with individuals who were involved with the case at the time, indicate a possible reasonable doubt that complete information on this occurrence was not available to the Investigating Committee. Also, it is somewhat unclear whether or not all steps of the grievance procedure were followed in this case.
>
> In view of these factors, we feel that a complete review of this grievance in the form of a hearing at which Captain Parker and others having information bearing on the case would be present, would be appropriate at this time. Sufficient questions seem now to have been raised to merit such a re-review. We would therefore suggest that we schedule a joint meeting between management and JSTOA representatives and that Captain Parker and others having pertinent information be invited to attend.
>
> If, as could be the case, full information was not available to the Accident Investigation Committee in its original review, we should be able in such a meeting now to settle this question once and for all. If you are agreeable, we would be happy to schedule it at the earliest time convenient.[14]

On September 29, 1971 a special meeting was held in New York. The assistant general manager, Mr. Sydney Wire, and the newly appointed employee relations manager for Marine, Captain Donald Graham, were present for the company. Two members of the association's executive committee and the association's adviser, plus the aggrieved party, Mr. Parker, and the master of the *Esso Florence,* Captain T. A. Johnson, also participated. Following the meeting the association was informed by letter dated October 6 and signed by the assistant general manager that:

> In reviewing the information presented at the meeting, there appears to me to be sufficient reasonable doubt about what actually happened to justify the revocation of Mr. Parker's suspension; consequently, I am directing that Mr. Parker be reimbursed for the pay withheld during the two weeks' suspension.
>
> Let me, however, emphasize again the importance of all officers' paying particular attention during vessel turnarounds to proper procedures that will insure no spillage of petroleum cargos. Such procedures are included in Marine regulations, circular letters, and in the recently issued Environmental Conservation manual for vessels.[15]

The understanding attitude of the company, even though it took two years for it to develop, might be considered a small victory for the association, but in a larger sense the case itself, as well as its outcome, did a number of things. Primarily, it established to the satisfaction of the membership the value to them of the association by effectively representing this member; secondly, it indicated a distaste for arbitration by the company (although shortly thereafter four unresolved grievances went this route) that necessitates submitting to outside judgment differences which, they believed, could and should be settled by the parties immediately involved; thirdly, because of the fleetwide attention given to the matter, all parties benefited by a better understanding of the continuing relation between the association and the company that went far beyond the immediate bargaining of an agreement; the company is less apt to act unilaterally in doubtful areas. And finally, at least in this case, there was a special dividend for all concerned, including the general public—a greater awareness among the fleet officers that the company *would not tolerate* carelessness or lack of concern where pollution was involved, regardless of quantity.

There have been grievances in other companies—Texaco, Mobil, and Getty. Some of these involved interpretation of the agreement, others have related to discipline. The latter have included suspension or discharge of officers where the company considered an infraction serious or where the conduct of an officer on watch was inconsistent with his responsibility. In several of these cases where the individual officer sought assistance from his association, reinstatement in the company or cancellation of the suspension was secured.

To secure reinstatement of a discharged officer requires reversing a management decision that has been taken only after long and careful deliberation—especially where the officer is a long-service employee. The management that authorized the discharge places itself in jeopardy should they reinstate that officer and he subsequently be the cause of an accident that involves large money losses or worse—loss of life. A decision to reinstate indeed is difficult in these circumstances. Nevertheless there have been several cases where a persistent plea for clemency has resulted in the reversal of the company's previous discharge decision. Where this involved an officer with considerable company service the decision was especially welcomed by the officer and his family.

To win a case where one feels there has been a miscarriage of justice is genuinely rewarding. To be able to restore a dismissed employee to his position when nothing but a plea for mercy can be employed brings far greater satisfaction. It is right to be just; it is ennobling to be merciful. When this occurs in the cold impersonal arena of the marketplace where competition almost requires a certain ruthlessness to survive, the quality of mercy is doubly ennobling; and places that management on a very special pedestal. The author is aware of such managements. Shakespeare's *Merchant of Venice* captures this virtue:

> But mercy is above the sceptered sway,
> It is enthroned in the hearts of kings,
> It is an attribute to God himself.

NOTES

1. Agreement, JSTOA and Marine Department, Humble Oil & Refining Company, March 13, 1970.
2. Arbitration, between Humble Oil & Refining Company and JSTOA, Antonio Rose, Grievant, May 16, 1972.
3. *Ibid.*
4. TTOA, *News Letter,* October 26, 1972.
5. Letter, to Master, *Esso Florence,* October 19, 1969, from Charles Parker, Chief Mate.
6. Letter, from Master, *Esso Florence* to Port Captain, Humble Oil & Refining Company, Houston, October 21, 1969.
7. Report, Company Investigating Committee, October 31, 1969.
8. Company Committee Recommendation to General Manager, Marine Department, November 10, 1969.
9. Letter, from Operations Manager to Charles Parker, December 2, 1969.
10. Letter, from Charles Parker to Operations Manager, Humble Oil & Refining Company, December 12, 1969.
11. Letter, from Charles Parker to General Manager, Humble Oil & Refining Company, December 15, 1969.

12. Letter, from Humble Oil & Refining Company to JSTOA, October 29, 1970.
13. Letter, from JSTOA to Humble Oil & Refining Company, June 9, 1971.
14. Letter, from Assistant General Manager, Humble Oil & Refining Company to JSTOA, August 9, 1971.
15. Letter, from Assistant General Manager, Humble Oil & Refining Company to JSTOA, October 6, 1971.

9

Seniority—Its Necessity and Its Fragility

PROBABLY NO SUBJECT STIRS UP MORE CONTROVERSY within an employee group than the role of strict seniority for promotion and demotion purposes. Management understandably wants the right to manage. But does the right to manage mean the right to move employees up and down at will, based on their alleged "fitness and ability" or their alleged lack of it? Volumes have been written containing diverse formulas for solving the dilemma and expanding arguments for and against these formulas.

Promotion or demotion based on strict seniority in the job is valued by the average employee especially as his length of service grows. It represents job protection. Admittedly, it is a negative approach in that it offers management little option when promotions are imminent. Nor does it offer the aggressive, above-average employee, especially if he is younger, an opportunity to advance on presumed merit.

The alternative to strict seniority would give management the right to promote or demote individual employees almost exclusively on their fitness and ability. The perennial difficulty with this approach is, of course, its inherent subjectivity. Who in management possesses such discernment and is so totally unbiased as to make a selection for promotion purely on merit? What yardsticks can be established as safe guidelines in arriving at so important a decision? While union members may fear for their job security, the issue is an emotional one on the company side of the table as well, for managers do in fact subject themselves to the harrowing process of promotion by merit and may be understandably envious of the system of mutually guaranteed promotions enjoyed by their ships' officers. It takes but one questionable decision on a promotion to upset the delicate balance among employees which we term morale. Even where it is grudgingly admitted that the individual promoted over others with greater seniority has demonstrated a greater competence, if the newly-promoted employee were related to the manager making the selection or if they attended the same school, go to the same church, or are members of the same fraternal organization—this becomes the reason for promotion, especially in the eyes of those passed over. Where there is serious doubt among his fellow employees that he is superior to them in fitness and ability, *and* where there is suspicion of favoritism connected with his promotion, a bitterness and cynicism can develop that can do incalculable damage among the remaining employees.

Among those major oil companies which bargain with independent unions for their seagoing employees, both seniority as an officer and fitness and ability are taken into consideration; but the emphasis is placed on seniority. However, should a licensed officer not secure a license at least one grade *higher than* that necessary to sail in a particular rank he is deemed to have failed to meet the fitness and ability yardstick. Also a series of unsatisfactory fitness reports could result in his being pegged in a position and being deemed not eligible for promotion, until such time as he demonstrated improvement. Demotions could be, and were, made, using the same yardstick.

Over the years and repeated in the 1970 Exxon agreement with the JSTOA is the following clause:

> ARTICLE VII (*a*) In all cases involving promotion or demotion length of service as an officer shall govern where fitness and ability are relatively equal. The final determination of fitness and ability must of necessity rest with the Company.
>
> (*b*) The Company agrees to continue its Rating Plan to assist in the determination of fitness and ability.[1]

Exxon provided the JSTOA with seniority lists both for deck officers and for engineers. These in turn were sent to the officers on the ships by the association. There was no secret as to the position of every officer in the fleet on the seniority list, and if an officer was not eligible at the time for promotion a mark alongside his name made this clear. Any movement therefore of an officer on the list that would cause him to "jump" his fellow officers immediately would become a cause for concern, especially among the officers over whom he advanced on the list.

There was a further refinement in the seniority provisions in the agreement between Exxon and the JSTOA. It involved transfers from seagoing to shoreside positions. In a company the size of Exxon there are many opportunities for officers to work in responsible positions ashore. The company has a large foreign-flag fleet, and much of the planning, logistics, and operation of that fleet is done by officers whose original employment was in the company's American-flag fleet. In addition there are a host of other shoreside positions for which seagoing officers may be qualified and which may interest them. This is healthy since it provides the company with experienced personnel for these assignments, and the seagoing officer has the knowledge that he is not necessarily restricted to going to sea for the rest of his company career. Finally, such movement of seagoing officers to shore assignments provides promotional opportunities for those who remain on the ships.

There remains one hitch, however. On occasion an officer who has transferred ashore returns to sea; and the question must be answered "What position on the seniority list should he occupy when he returns?" The Exxon agreement attempted to anticipate such a situation by providing in its seniority policy as follows:

> An officer transferred to the shore payroll of Esso Shipping Company, Esso Standard Oil Company, or any of their affiliated companies will retain his seniority rating during this period. However, he will not advance beyond the top of the rank in which he was listed at the time of transfer. Officers who may be advanced over him when he has reached the top of the rank will retain their position ahead of him if downward adjustments are necessary due to curtailment of fleet activities. Credit for pay purposes will be given to the same extent as for seniority.[2]

The seagoing seniority status of officers who return to sea after periods of shore-based employment also had arisen in the Texaco fleet. In one instance an officer who had taken a shore position decided to return to sea after having been ashore for twelve years. Placed in the rank which he had held prior to going ashore he adversely affected the position on the seniority list of those beneath him. They were stepped back one number. This became highly controversial.[3] It did little good to remind the affected officers that during the period this officer had been ashore they had stepped up. In theory, and perhaps in practice, it may be better to have been up and down than never to have been up at all, but the mere fact of an officer's returning to sea who has been ashore for a considerable period irks those who had remained at sea. Many seamen are especially suspicious of shoreside sailors and envious of their supposedly happy home life. And when they are adversely affected in their seniority listing by one who returns to their fold from shoreside, they consider this to be grossly unfair.

To remedy this in part, Texaco and the TTOA during the 1972 bargaining sessions negotiated the following change in the clause relating to continuous service and seniority:

> Officers who take shore positions shall retain their seniority position at the time they came ashore for a period of five years. During this period no promotional seniority shall accrue.
> An officer who returns to the bargaining unit after the lapse of five consecutive years shall drop to the bottom of the promotional list on which he was listed at the time of the transfer.
> However, if fleet reductions occur within this time the officer who had been ashore shall not return to the fleet in a position above the officer who was above him at the time he went ashore.
> The above shall not affect the status of officers who attend special schools for periods of time in the interest of the Company.[4]

This clause mollified most of the Texaco officers who considered the previous arrangement too favorable for the officer who went ashore and later returned to sea.

In the light of the attention focused by seagoing officers on the seniority list and their position on it, the return to sea in Exxon of a particular officer who had been ashore for a lengthy period brought the matter of the seniority status for officers in that company who came ashore and subsequently returned to sea into sharp relief. In this instance, however, there was an important difference: The particular officer's period ashore could be divided into (1) service to the ships requiring the officer's Merchant Seaman's Document issued by the Coast Guard, and (2) strict shore service where such document was not required. The officer involved, Louis Staar, had been ashore more than four years. His return to sea affected a number of officers who because of the seniority position assigned to him had to step back one number.

In possible anticipation of his return to sea, Staar earlier had sought a ruling from the association regarding his shore status as it affected his seagoing seniority. His letter was written after he had been ashore for a year and a half.

> Dear Sirs:
> In February of 1966 I accepted a job ashore. My primary duty is, and has been, assisting the Chief Mates in the loading of the "Esso Houston" and the "Esso New Orleans" at Baton Rouge

and Baytown. Approximately 120 hours of my working time per month has been occupied in this pursuit.

In the interest of myself and others who may follow me (hopefully) in similar shore positions, I would appreciate a ruling as to whether this job should entail the same frozen seniority provisions as other shore positions.

In the performance of my duties I have full authority to take charge of the deck watch as directed by the Chief Mate, assuming the same responsibilities as if attached to the ship.

As to whatever value my presence aboard these ships has been I refer you to the Chief Mates with whom I have been working: Carl Lohman, Arthur Smith, Dan Bradley, Torrance Inman, George Beck, Jack Morrell.

I feel that our agreement should be modified to cover the seniority of mates assigned to assist in cargo handling. I am not aware of any other tanker company that requires mates whose primary function is assisting in cargo handling aboard ship to return to sea to maintain their seniority status.

Hopefully, it will not be necessary for me to return to sea to maintain my seniority—not only from my standpoint, but that of those below me that would sail in a lower rating.

Very truly yours,
Louis H. Staar[5]

The association did not meet this issue squarely at the time since it would have meant modifying the seniority policy to meet a very special situation. Furthermore, it was assumed Staar would not be returning to sea. The association's reply therefore simply referred to the basic seniority policy as applied to officers who return to sea after a shore assignment.

Subsequent to his letter Staar was assigned to a clearly defined shore position at the company's office in Houston, Texas. He served in this capacity for a little more than two years and then returned to sea. At this time the company placed him on the seagoing seniority list in accordance with the terms of the agreement between the company and the JSTOA.

But this was not satisfactory to him. Staar reminded the association that during part of the time he had been ashore his work was aboard ships in port for which his seagoing license was required. The association therefore brought this matter to the attention of the company in a grievance meeting held on November 30, 1971. In their reply to the association's contention the management wrote:

In response to the association's request and because of the unusual nature of this case, we have adjusted Mr. Staar's position on the Operating Seniority List. His new position is between Messrs. Brower and Haugevik. When Mr. Staar began his assignment at Baytown on February 1, 1966 he was on the Third Mate's list between Messrs. Kirby and Falvo. Therefore, on September 14, 1968 when Mr. Staar completed this assignment he would have been immediately behind Mr. Kirby on the Second Mate's list had this assignment been treated as sea service.

From September 15, 1968 to November 16, 1970 Mr. Staar was on an assignment in Houston which is not considered to be sea service. During this period had he been immediately behind Mr. Kirby on the list, he would have been passed over by Messrs. Falvo, Milligan, Brelsford, Ewell, Fellows, and Brower. We assume that you will inform Mr. Staar and the other nineteen individuals involved of this affirmative answer to your request.[6]

When the decision of the company agreeing with the association's position was relayed to the fleet, the fur began to fly. Minutes of a meeting held aboard the *Esso Philadelphia* dated February 7 were received by the association with a request that they be circulated to the fleet as received. The deck officers were furious when they learned of the adjustment in the seniority position of Mr. Staar. We quote from the ship's minutes.

A meeting of the membership was called this day at 10:00 A.M., to discuss at length the filtered down story that Mr. Lou Staar has been readjusted on the Seniority List to his "rightful position?". This came as no surprise. On December 6 last, Mr. Bertram Christensen boarded this vessel in Boston and informed us that the association's executive committee was at that time working for an adjustment. . . .

What threats, or promises, could the company use to coerce the committee into such a foolhardy undertaking; one that would jeopardize their good standing throughout the fleet? FACT or FICTION. Certainly an explanation is in order—and immediate steps taken to rectify a gross injustice. Why penalize those who stayed at sea for eight years—carrying the "pay load" and the Lou Staars, because of their failure to acquire the proper manner in which to hold a cocktail glass?

The committee has talked and preached manning scale and job security for the last several years. The SENIORITY LIST is our job security, and it is now being threatened. Where DO you stand? Therefore, in view of the fact that the executive committee has always worked for the good of the whole, we hesitate to believe the rumors, and await anxiously for their explanation.

There can be no denial on anyone's part that Mr. Staar's RIGHT-FUL position is at the top of the Third Mate's List—and that his advance off that list must come from normal attrition. Any attempt to alter this policy and to install Mr. Staar in that position recently vacated by Mr. Roy Berg will NOT be tolerated.

We are prepared to have a copy of this printed and circulated ourselves.

Fraternally yours,

WILLIAM DUNDON, *Ch. Engr.*	DAVIS ABERNATHY, *Master*
FRED SCHULER, *1st Asst.*	GERALD F. SMITH, *Ch. Mate*
EUGENE STUBBLEFIELD, *2nd Asst.*	DAVID WHITTY, *Third Mate*[7]
HOWARD OTTMAN, *3rd Asst.*	
ED LARSON, *Extra Third Asst.*	

The minutes of the *Esso Philadelphia* had to be circulated. This was the policy of the JSTOA. However, the executive committee felt the fleet was entitled to know the full story and be given a chance to comment and so the following was inserted immediately following the minutes:

Now that you have read the letter the committee feels that an explanation is due the entire fleet as there appears to be some misunderstanding as to just what did happen and why it happened in the case of Lou Staar's seniority. An effort was made to do this in an Editor's Note which appeared on page 7 of the *News Letter* dated February 9, 1972 (Vol. 72, No. 2).

No member of the executive committee stands to gain or lose by any decision regarding the seniority of Lou Staar. The executive committee is elected by the membership not only to bargain agreements but to handle grievances and do one hundred and one other things that the membership may desire from time to time.

Seniority cases are by their very nature sticky ones. No matter what decision is made somebody gains and somebody loses. Over the years efforts have been made to write into the agreement a basic seniority policy. However, no matter how well a policy is written there always seems to develop a case which does not fit the policy.

Lou Staar came ashore in February 1966. He came ashore to assist Chief Mates in the loading of the "Esso Houston" and "Esso New Orleans" at Baton Rouge and Baytown. His license was required to perform this work and the very job itself was created as a result of the efforts of the association to secure an additional mate on these vessels. The company would not agree to this but subsequently established the job that Lou Staar did, namely, that of assisting in the loading of these vessels.

On August 29, 1967 he wrote to the association explaining his job and asking them for a ruling regarding his seagoing seniority. While he was ashore individuals who were on the seniority list below him moved up. Now that he has returned to sea in effect these individuals moved back. It was felt by the executive committee upon the request of Lou Staar that the company should be approached to determine whether or not because of the nature of his duties in assisting in the loading of these vessels he should not be given sea service credit. After much review and going back into the records, etc., the company finally agreed and in their agreement Mr. Staar was not given seagoing seniority credit for *all* of the time he was ashore, but *only* during the period from February 1, 1966 to September 14, 1968. The remaining time that Mr. Staar spent ashore he has not been given credit for seagoing seniority.

Faced with this type of case we would like to ask the membership what would your decision be and we are enclosing an open type of reply but will even go to a secret ballot if the membership so desires.

As we have said above, seniority cases are sticky at best and disastrous at worst. You are damned if you do and damned if you don't. So maybe by giving all the facts to the membership, the membership can tell the committee what they would like the committee to do. We are not God nor are we trying to play God. We are trying to do the best job we can for all the members both individually and collectively.

If we have made a mistake in a particular case, tell us if you would like to have it handled differently and we will endeavor to follow your desires.

Your Executive Committee

DWAINE HETTINGER
FRANK STODDARD
JOHN MURPHY
BERTRAM CHRISTENSEN[8]

The ballot sent to the fleet read "Do you believe the executive committee did the right thing as far as credit for seagoing seniority is concerned in the case of Lou Staar?"

The vote was 76 to 32 to support the action taken by the executive committee.[9] While those who had to step back one number were not happy, at least the association was supported in a position they believed equitable in so sensitive an area as seniority listing on a promotional list. While similar individual grievance cases settled on the local level can be cited by national unions, it must be borne in mind that, where bargaining itself is done on the local level, the likelihood of such a grievance becoming the cause of a wildcat strike or a local strike approved and supported by the national union not only is remote, but just does not exist. Relief, if the local union feels there is an inequity, can be sought in the arbitration clause (agreed to by the parties when the contract itself was negotiated); in Exxon this has been invoked in a few instances.

NOTES

1. Agreement, JSTOA and Humble Oil & Refining Company, March 13, 1970.
2. *Ibid.*
3. Texaco, *Official Records.*
4. Agreement, TTOA and Texaco Inc., September 1, 1972.
5. Letter, Louis Staar to JSTOA, August 29, 1967.
6. Letter, Humble Oil & Refining Company to JSTOA, January 10, 1972.
7. Letter (Minutes of Meeting), *Esso Philadelphia* to JSTOA, February 7, 1972.
8. JSTOA, *News Letter,* February 9, 1972.
9. JSTOA *Official Records, 1972.*

10

A Wide Range of Interests

THE RANGE OF ITEMS AFFECTING EMPLOYEES both as individuals and in groups represented in local-level bargaining by independent unions encompasses anything, from taking a position on compulsory arbitration to arguing for more government concern in strengthening the American Merchant Marine.

COMPULSORY ARBITRATION NOT THE ANSWER

Apart from handling specific grievances, there are other matters that may only indirectly affect the members of local-level bargaining units but nevertheless are of concern to them. Some are not immediate, and seem almost abstruse as far as their effect on current bargaining is concerned. Such was the effort by forces within government and certain maritime-industry groups (not tankers) in the spring of 1963 to secure legislation that would have required compulsory arbitration in maritime labor disputes. The unhappy strike record of this industry cried out for relief. Some saw this relief in compulsory arbitration. No doubt in the light of the labor history in the maritime industry since the end of World War II many sincerely believed there must be a better way than the 38 strikes involving seamen alone that had taken place between 1945 and 1963.[1] That was the reason for the proposed compulsory arbitration. And it was an inviting proposal to many congressmen.

But quick solutions are not only not lasting many times, but more importantly, if achieved by compulsion rather than by agreement, they can destroy the delicate fabric that shields a free society from the servile one. The author as adviser to the several independent unions in the tanker segment of the maritime industry appeared before the House Committee on Merchant Marine and Fisheries to oppose the bill which would have given the President the right to invoke compulsory arbitration in major maritime labor–management disputes.

After reciting the enviable record of independent tanker unions that in their more than 25 years of existence had never caused or participated in a work stoppage in the maritime industry, he testified:

> Bargaining at best is difficult. It's time-consuming and, to some people, almost frustrating. But it is a small price indeed to pay for freedom.
>
> Compulsory arbitration, no matter how fancy its dress, and no matter how attractive it may seem to some people, is the *elimination of freedom*. It is giving over to some third party the right to determine wages and working conditions. It is the antithesis of free collective bargaining.
>
> Regardless of how able the arbitrator may be (and how does one judge an arbitrator's ability?) in a sense *he is not a responsible person*—certainly not in the same sense that a union is responsible to its members or a management is responsible to its stockholders.
>
> Those individuals in management who have come before this Committee and have urged the passage of this Bill long ago lost direct contact with their employees. Apparently they feel they cannot be any worse off than they are now by having compulsory arbitration. This is capitulation with a capital "C." Mussolini made the trains run on time, and the Italian people lost their liberty. Hitler eliminated strikes in Germany; he also eliminated people. Since 1917 Russia has *planned* for its people—where they work, what they eat, who they can be with, and how much they are paid; and, with frightening frequency, when they die. And they have no strikes.
>
> No matter how serious a strike, no matter how long a strike, no matter how much inconvenience a strike may bring, and no matter what the financial and other losses may be, it still is a small price to pay for freedom.
>
> Merely because some companies have found it painful, embarrassing, or difficult to utilize whatever protection the law may give them in free collective bargaining and whatever economic muscle they can muster is no reason to foist on an entire industry an ironclad compulsory arbitration provision.
>
> Many in the United States today are concerned about the gradual chipping away at their individual liberties. Many are concerned with the growing power of government—federal, state, and local. Any increase in this power becomes an increase in the power of government *over* the people, despite the fact that it may be written in language indicating that it is *for* the people.

Congress itself is being eclipsed day after day by the executive branch of the government. This Bill, if it became law, would add still further to the powers of the executive branch of the Federal Government which becomes an automatic encroachment on the legislative branch. Regardless of its high purposes, this Bill represents regulation. In the opinion of many this nation already is too far down the road toward strangulation by regulation.

Once a wrong principle is established, nothing but wrong can flow from it. In a free country, the principle of government compulsion in bargaining is wrong. Ultimately that compulsion is carried out by the government at the point of a bayonet—because the bayonet is merely the extension of the force involved in giving the government such extraordinary power in the first place.

As you know, while independent unions represent but a small segment of the industry—namely, seagoing personnel employed by several major oil companies—we believe we have demonstrated without a shadow of a doubt over a long period, in both war and peace, that successful bargaining can be accomplished, that economic benefits can accrue to the men who man the ships, and that companies can operate without interruption, if a serious effort is made to do this.

We hold no brief for those unfortunate companies who have perhaps found that their past callousness toward their employees has earned for themselves the difficulties and the disabilities under which they undoubtedly operate, from the standpoint of satisfactory labor relations. Their plight, however, should not plunge this industry, and later other industries, into the dark unknown of arbitration, accomplished by highly respected professors with feet planted firmly in mid-air.[2]

It would be immodest to think that this adverse testimony was at all telling, but it was good to learn later that the compulsory arbitration bill was shelved.

Where, as in many contracts, arbitration is provided, it is something that the parties have *agreed to,* and it involves interpretations of the basic agreement that was freely negotiated. This is a far cry from compulsory arbitration regarding what goes into an agreement.

WHITHER AMERICAN-FLAG SHIPS?

While the word "whither" in the above title questions the future of American-flag ships, the same word without the first "h" could in large measure describe the course of American shipping since

World War II—it has continued to wither. Those dealing with the economics of shipping say we have priced ourselves off the ocean. But American interests, especially the major oil companies, have larger tanker fleets than ever. And although their current American-flag vessels compare favorably—in tonnage—with their pre-World War II fleet, except for some inroads by the Colonial Pipe Line, the number of their foreign-flag vessels carrying petroleum, especially crude oil, to United States ports from foreign ports has reached substantial proportions.

The international oil companies have chosen Panama and Liberia as the countries under whose flags they feel it is both profitable and safe to sail their vessels. These flags have been dubbed by opponents of this practice "flags of convenience." Those who use these flags have replied that they are "flags of necessity." Generally speaking the Department of Defense considers that, because these vessels are not under the flags of major maritime nations, and since their crews comprise nationals of a variety of countries and the direction of their operations is from United States-based major oil companies, the United States from a defense posture has "effective control" of them should hostilities require their employment.

This "flight from the flag" remains a continuing source of irritation, both to those who make their careers sailing in American-flag vessels and to those countless Americans whose pride in their country and concern for her protection is more than a passing fad. In July 1961 Jorgen Jahre, President of the Norwegian Shipowners Association, declared that vessels registered under "flags of convenience" * would be less dependable at an outbreak of war for use by the North Atlantic Treaty Organization (NATO) than vessels under Allied flags. Stating that he did not "doubt the willingness of American owners to make such vessels available," Mr. Jahre said that, unlike Allied vessels, "the officers and seamen on PanLibHon ships do not owe allegiance to the land of the flag, in most cases, nor to the country where the vessels are beneficially owned." [3] Defending the continuance of the practice of using "flags of convenience" vessels (or "flags of necessity"), a study made by the National Academy of Sciences and the National Research Council concluded:

---

* Ships registered in Panama, Liberia, and Honduras are collectively called "flags of convenience" by opponents of this practice.

> The crews of ships under PanLibHon flags are all nationals of countries friendly to the United States. The majority are nationals of NATO countries. On the outbreak of an emergency, ships would be routed to selected points for proper screening of personnel—and replacement where appropriate. Dependent upon individual ship locations on the outbreak of an emergency, it is possible that some of the foreign crews may defect and deliver a few PanLibHon ships into enemy hands. In the event of a NATO war it is also possible that some European crews may ignore the orders of U. S. shipowners and deliver ships to ports of the countries from which they were employed. In the latter case, such ships would still support the common NATO effort and their employment would be governed by NATO pooling and location procedures.[4]

A test of what seamen on these vessels might do should all-out war occur has yet to be made. Meanwhile educated guesses are being made by both sides to the controversy.

During the 1961 seamen's strike, which in large measure was aimed at major oil companies with large fleets under the flags of Panama and Liberia, President Kennedy invoked the Taft-Hartley Act. At a press conference during the strike the President, after noting that "ships are put by American owners under other flags in order to avoid paying the wage scale which we have for our American Merchant Marine," warned "This is a competitive business. We could very well find instead of flags of convenience or so-called runaway ships that it, the strike, would actually put some under flags of, or in contractual relationship with, the British or the Norwegians, and then we would not have the control in case of a national emergency, and *still be undercut.*" [5]

Many feel that a little ingenuity by major oil companies plus a more sympathetic attitude by Congress to overall American interests and more understanding by seagoing labor of the economic disparities that exist between American costs and foreign costs would provide a basis for the maintenance of a more viable American Merchant Marine. Independent unions representing personnel employed aboard American-flag tankers of the major oil companies repeatedly have gone on record with suggested solutions. As early as 1954 in a lengthy petition to Congress these independent unions argued that a portion of petroleum transported from foreign ports should be carried in American-flag vessels:

> In our opinion, in this mixed-up political world of ours, it is pretty difficult to tell what nation is going to be your friend and what

nation is going to be your enemy, almost from month to month. But even if it could be definitely established that the Panama and Liberian fleets were assured to the U. S. because of the friendly attitude of their governments, what about the seamen who man these ships? Where do their loyalties lie today and where will they lie tomorrow and the day after tomorrow?[6]

At that time M. G. Gamble, President of Esso Shipping Company, testified before the Senate Subcommittee on Merchant Marine and Fisheries:

> . . . only with foreign-flag registry and foreign crews can tankers be competitive in trade not restricted by law to U. S. flag. Under this circumstance the choice is not between our flag and a foreign flag but only between various foreign flags. Panama, where ships will be available to the U. S. in times of emergency on American terms, seems to us to be the best choice when other circumstances do not dictate a different flag.[7]

Specifically, the independent unions in the tanker industry have sought legislation that would require a portion of petroleum coming from foreign lands to be transported in American-flag tankers. Letters on the subject have been addressed to Presidents Eisenhower, Kennedy, and Nixon, always with the objective of enlisting executive support for some form of protection for American-flag tankers.[8] To date, none of these efforts has been productive. The matter continues to be reviewed, discussed, and argued, but still no solution.

In a thirty-seven-page article entitled "Flags of Necessity, Flags of Convenience, or Runaway Ships?" Professor Edward B. Shils of the Wharton School of Finance and Commerce, University of Pennsylvania, states:

> The concerted effort of the United States maritime unions to organize the "run-away" ships has led to an increase in the number of such ships which have been placed under the British flags, rather than the PanLibHon flags. In 1959 American shipowners of foreign-flag ships placed only 9.7 per cent of their investments under the British flag. In 1961 the British flag accounted for 36.9 per cent of the overall investments of shipowners.
>
> American owners, fearing organization of PanLibHon ships, are beginning to either lease or sell their vessels to oldline seafaring nations such as England. Whether these ships will be available when the United States Government needs them as has been stated in the situation with registration in Liberia, remains to be seen. Will we witness a continuation of "forced sales"?[9]

On May 8, 1961, the independent tanker associations appealed to President Kennedy, as they previously had appealed to President Eisenhower, to support legislation that would strengthen the American Merchant Marine. In their letter they stated:

> If it were possible to provide, by law, or otherwise for an *international wage* the unfair competition that presently prevails between foreign-flag ships and American-flag ships largely would be removed. To hope for such an international wage, however, is wishful thinking. It never has been done, and there is no reason, based on the realities, to believe it ever will be—although operating subsidies granted in special situations help meet the wage inequity. . . .
>
> Mr. President, the principle of prudence in protecting a national resource as vital as our ocean-going transportation should urge you to take appropriate action now. There is danger in delay. These are days of decision. Each decision in the present struggle for the survival of our nation and the free world can be the difference between victory and defeat. Ships—the bridge of merchant ships—spelled that difference in World War II.[10]

On May 23 the associations received a reply to their letter to President Kennedy. Acting Under-Secretary for Transportation, Frank L. Barton, replied for the President. His letter contained no new hope that anything specific would be done to bring about the kind of help the associations sought. Instead, Barton went over the same ground that the Eisenhower Administration officials had covered—continuing to oppose legislative relief:

> To require the transportation of commercial cargoes in American-flag ships would represent a major shift in United States policy which could have serious repercussions in the form of trade restriction throughout the free world.
>
> . . . The problems of the American Merchant Marine, including the question of greater U. S.-flag participation in the United States foreign trade, is now under study on a broad front. The objective is to define more clearly the critical problem areas, and to seek acceptable solutions to them. I can assure you that every effort is being made to find ways by which our maritime industries can be made more efficient in meeting world competition.[11]

The difficulty in maintaining an adequate American Merchant Marine, and doing so within the bounds of a free economy, seems insuperable. The overtones of international commerce, which is highly competitive, added to the political considerations which always must be kept in mind, pose problems that the government and the industry have been facing, but without marked success, since World War II. From a national viewpoint, the "flight from the flag" must be evaluated in the light of its impact on national defense. What suitable alternative can be devised to meet the growing uncertainty with respect to the "availability" to the United States, in case of war, of vessels registered under the PanLibHon flags; and finally what will happen if the majority of ships currently under PanLibHon flags are transferred to such maritime nations as Norway, Greece, or Great Britain?

On January 5, 1972, the adviser to the tanker independents wrote to President Nixon, saying in part:

> We feel the time has come again to emphasize to you as the Chief Executive of this nation how imperative it is to maintain the American Merchant Marine. We are familiar with your efforts to provide for a ten-year building program to revamp and rehabilitate the American-flag fleet. But ships without cargoes are like ships without rudders.
>
> We are cognizant of the various meetings that have been held in Washington by the Federal Maritime Board and the Hearings that have taken place before the House Committee on Merchant Marine and Fisheries regarding the plight of the American Merchant Marine. Most of these are depressing. Solutions suggested are either unrealistic, exceedingly costly, or both.
>
> Subsidies as such are not necessarily the answer to a viable American Merchant Marine. What is necessary in our opinion is a *firm commitment* that a portion of petroleum coming to the United States by vessel *come in American-flag vessels.* You, as the Chief Executive of this nation, can bring this about. This is a matter of vital concern not just to the American Merchant Marine as a service but to the very defense of the United States as a nation.
>
> We stated our position on this matter during President Eisenhower's Administration and during President Kennedy's Administration. Perhaps the importance of this was not readily recognized then but today we find time running out. As you repeatedly have said, "We must be strong—not to take advantage of others but to protect ourselves." [12]

To leave no stone unturned, letters were sent by the tanker independents to the board chairmen of several of the major oil companies in July of 1972. They urged that, apart from legislative action, major oil companies should on their own devise ways and means to meet the growing criticism voiced by Americans of the increasing use of foreign-flag tankers to carry petroleum to the United States—petroleum that in one form or another would be consumed *in* the United States.[13]

Rawleigh Warner, Jr., Board Chairman of Mobil, indicated sympathy for the objectives sought by the tanker independents, but in his response maintained that they at best could be achieved on a voluntary, rather than a mandatory, basis:

> I can assure you that Mobil's management is fully cognizant of the situation to which you refer and is very much involved in discussions related to proposed legislation now under consideration by the Congress of the United States. We have established a definitive corporate policy with respect to supporting the principle of increased utilization of U. S.-flag tankers and have consistently advocated such a program. However, we firmly believe that any long-term program such as this can only be effectively implemented on a voluntary rather than a mandatory basis under provisions that will provide utilization of such vessels at a competitive cost.[14]

All major oil companies opposed Senate Bill S.3404 which would have mandated that half the crude oil imported into the United States be carried on American-flag vessels. This was an amendment to the House Bill H.R. 13324, a Maritime Subsidy Authorization Bill. Arguments used against such mandated imports were:

> It would launch the U. S. on a course of rampant protectionism certain to provoke damaging retaliation from other countries. It would saddle the American consumer with inflationary increases in the costs of the energy he uses. It would create a non-competitive captive market for transporting half of the commercial crude-oil cargoes coming to this country, while opening the way for a labor dispute to apply a stranglehold to a major portion of the nation's fuel supply.[15]

In conversations between this author and the general manager of the Marine Transportation Department of Mobil, subsequently reduced in part to writing, Mobil's position in opposition to the particular legislation was amplified.

> I would hope that my outline of Mobil's position, evaluations and actions, related to the proposed Congressional legislation, will provide you with the full assurance that Mobil's objectives and those of the Tanker Officers Association "run a parallel course." However, we do feel, for all of the reasons I explained to you,

that the legislation presently under consideration by Subcommittees of the House of Representatives and the U. S. Senate is not the proper method of establishing or implementing an effective program.

This corporation has established a position of leadership through being identified with the formulation, submission, and recommendation to all appropriate government agencies, of a specific commercially acceptable alternate approach which would permit construction of tankers in the United States, to be manned by U. S. crews and utilized in foreign trade.[16]

From this it could be hoped that help is on the way; but there still are many important details to be worked out. The proposed legislation, Senate Bill S.3404, failed passage with New England Senators Kennedy and Muskie, among others, voting for its defeat. New England, a heavy consumer of heating oil, currently is complaining about the disparity in heating-oil prices for that part of the country compared with the rest of the nation. Required importation of a portion of petroleum in American-flag vessels would increase further the price to the consumer, argued Senators Kennedy and Muskie. The solution to the problem has not yet surfaced.

Whether ultimately it will be solely by legislative act, executive order, entirely by voluntary approaches (with an ear to the ground for consumer reaction, nationalist feelings, and concern for a guarantee of supply), or through a combination of these—the problem will not go away. And with the energy situation becoming more critical each year, more people are beginning to realize how important it is not to be a captive of foreign oil or foreign-flag ships (including flags of convenience). This is one of the overriding reasons for approval of the long-delayed Alaskan pipeline. In an attempt to clarify the energy crisis, Rawleigh Warner, Jr., Mobil Board Chairman, in the June 11, 1973 issue of *NAM Reports* (a publication of the National Association of Manufacturers) stated:

> We know we must have superports, onshore or offshore or both, able to accommodate not only the very large crude carriers already in service but also the still larger ones being built. . . .
> *We know we must begin to develop a U. S.-flag tanker fleet* that can be competitive in world trade, to ease the balance-of-payments drain that will arise from massive imports of a commodity involving a large transportation cost. . . .[17]

Such a public pronouncement by the chairman of the board of a major international oil company could well be that necessary first move to mobilize Congress and the maritime administration to devise the machinery to have this hope become a reality.

International oil companies both directly and through the American Petroleum Institute continue to oppose any cargo-preference legislation. In December 1973 the latter organization stated their objections in a brief, entitled "The Cargo Preference Issue." [18] In it they argued that "cargo preference legislation will directly result in higher transportation costs because (1) U. S. vessels will cost more when operating in a captive market, (2) foreign governments will retaliate, and (3) the entire marine transportation system will become less flexible." [19] They insist that "the total cumulative cost of such legislation between now and 1985 is estimated to be approximately $22 billion. This is compared to an estimate of about $7 billion for a similar expansion under the provisions of the Merchant Marine Act." [20] This act, generally termed the Merchant Marine Act of 1970, represents amendments to the original Merchant Marine Act of 1936. It is intended to provide more encouragement to private industry to build and operate American-flag ships.

According to the American Petroleum Institute statement, "In 1972 the 18.3 million deadweight tons under effective U. S. control [ships under Panamanian, Liberian, and Honduran flags] plus the 7 million deadweight tons of the U. S. fleet could have covered over ninety-eight per cent of the total tonnage requirements, including domestic trades, grain, MSC [Military Sea Cargoes], and all petroleum import requirements." [21]

Clearly the bulk of these U. S. tonnage requirements are being met by the "flags of convenience" ships. The fear of the major international oil companies is that cargo-preference legislation will force U. S. companies to "curtail the size of their effective controlled fleets, replacing Panamanian- and Liberian-flag tankers with tankers registered in and controlled by other foreign countries," thereby sacrificing both the economies and the U. S. effective control which, they maintain, currently exists. This is why the subsidy approach is favored.

However, the subsidy approach does not at present represent clear sailing for major American oil companies with foreign-flag fleets. The reason is that *operating* subsidies can be obtained only if the Maritime Administration waives the so-called grandfather clause, or if Congress eliminates this requirement. The grandfather clause precludes a company with a foreign fleet from receiving an operating subsidy. At the moment, the Maritime Administration has been unwilling to grant such a waiver. This is not a problem, however, with respect to *construction* subsidies.

Exxon and several other companies recently received approval for *construction* subsidies to build six 400,000-ton tankers. These, when completed, will be the largest American-flag ships afloat. With respect to these vessels the *operating* subsidy is of minor importance. Their size provides built-in economic advantages that far outweigh the wage differential that exists between wages paid to American seamen and those paid to foreign seamen. These ships, designated ULCC (ultra-large cargo carriers), plus planned offshore superports to handle them, will go a long way toward making the United States Merchant Marine more competitive, especially in the transportation of petroleum.

In respect to the present restrictions regarding operating subsidies which make major American oil companies with foreign-flag fleets ineligible for such subsidies, several of the independent tanker associations are currently investigating the possibility of having this restriction lifted. This possibly could be accomplished by having the Maritime Administration waive this restriction where an American oil company agreed to man any newly constructed Panamanian- and/or Liberian-flag vessels with American officers. While this would be somewhat more costly to the American oil companies, if as a result of such agreement they could be assured of operating subsidies for newly constructed American-flag vessels it might be an attractive trade-off. Furthermore, the manning of these vessels with American officers would strengthen effective U. S. control of this currently substantial foreign-flag fleet.

The May 1972 edition of the *Annals* of the American Academy of Political and Social Science contains a comprehensive overview of the relations between the United States and the Middle East with more than passing emphasis on the role played by the vast oil reserves in this region. A better understanding of the magnitude and importance of these reserves can be had in the light of recently programed energy needs of the United States. However, reserves without production and transportation are of little value. Thomas C. Barger, Chief Executive Officer from 1961 until his retirement in 1969 of the Arabian American Oil Company (comprised of four major oil companies) contributed an article to the *Annals* entitled "Middle Eastern Oil since the Second World War." [22] In this Barger stated:

> In my experience, few people outside the oil industry fully grasp the vastness of the quantities of oil handled daily. For example,

the 2½ billion tons now produced and used annually are more than the world's annual tonnage of food production. But, as contrasted with most foodstuffs and other raw materials, oil is rather difficult and expensive to store. Because of this characteristic, less than a three-month supply of world oil is above ground at any one time. Consequently, as the use of oil is continuous, enormous volumes are at all times flowing from the wells to the refineries and to the consumer who is dependent on this constant and uninterrupted flow to keep him going, whether he is running a power plant or a motorcycle.

Most of the oil in export trade is transported by sea. The quantities transported are now so great that half of the world's merchant fleet is composed of oil tankers.

The United States, a net exporter of oil in 1946, now imports some 3⅔ million barrels per day (bpd) of crude oil and products. The imports would be much greater were it not for our oil policy which limits imports by a quota system so as to hold the domestic price of oil high enough to encourage exploration and to keep a large part of the domestic industry in being.*

With this information, and much more is available, on the need for tanker transportation, the question of how much petroleum shall be carried in American-flag tankers can better be answered.

It would be presumptuous to claim that this transportation problem can be solved by and with the advice of independent tanker associations. But surely their record of uninterrupted service is a strong argument for a more penetrating study of how these American-flag vessels can be utilized to carry the crude from the source of supply to the consumer centers in the United States. Congress and/or the Maritime Administration must help—but in a manner consonant with the competitive needs of major oil companies, protection of American consumers and taxpayers from the increasing encroachment on their pocketbooks, and security of supply for America's energy needs and national defense.

As this manuscript is being readied for publication new legislative efforts to assist American-flag tankers are being made. Encouraged by reports of pending bills to provide a portion of petroleum coming from foreign ports to be carried in American-flag ships, several independent tanker associations sent telegrams to Chairman Leonor K. Sullivan, Committee on Merchant Marine

---

* On May 7, 1973, oil import quotas were ended because of the current fuel shortage. This was several months prior to the oil embargo by Arab oil-producing states.

and Fisheries, U. S. House of Representatives. The telegrams in effect were a repeat of a position taken by these associations for almost twenty years. In part they said:

> THIS ASSOCIATION WISHES TO GO ON RECORD AS SUPPORTING THE BARRETT BILL REQUIRING A PORTION OF PETROLEUM COMING FROM FOREIGN TO BE CARRIED IN AMERICAN FLAG VESSELS. WE WISH FURTHER TO STATE THAT WE ARE IN FAVOR OF THIS BILL OR ANY SIMILAR BILL INTRODUCED BY ANY OTHER MEMBER OF THE HOUSE OF REPRESENTATIVES THAT WILL PROVIDE FOR A PORTION OF PETROLEUM COMING FROM FOREIGN TO BE CARRIED IN AMERICAN FLAG VESSELS. THIS POSITION WAS TAKEN BY THIS ASSOCIATION TOGETHER WITH OTHER INDEPENDENT TANKER UNIONS AS LONG AGO AS 1954 BOTH BY PETITIONS TO CONGRESS AS WELL AS BY INDIVIDUAL COMMUNICATIONS TO PRESIDENTS EISENHOWER, KENNEDY, AND NIXON. WE ARE PLEASED TO LEARN THAT APPARENTLY REAL PROGRESS IS BEING MADE TOWARD THE ACHIEVEMENT OF THIS GOAL.

A prompt reply was received from Congresswoman Sullivan which at this writing indicates that there is light at the end of the tunnel and that the tunnel is getting shorter.

July 5, 1973

This is in reply to a number of telegrams received from various tanker officers associations concerning legislation which would require that a percentage of petroleum products imported into the United States must come in on U. S.-flag vessels.

As the members of the associations probably know, a number of bills have been introduced recently relating to percentage of carriage on U. S.-flag bottoms of imported petroleum products. On May 29, 1973, I sponsored H.R. 8193, together with 23 co-sponsors, which would require a percentage of petroleum products coming into the U. S. to be carried on American-flag vessels. All of the bills which have been introduced in the House are identical. As of this time our Committee has not scheduled any hearings on this matter.

In the last Congress the Senate considered similar legislation which was defeated by a vote of 41 to 33. Since this type of legislation was not able to pass the Congress in the last session, we would like some indication as to its future before we take it up in Committee. For this reason, we will await action by the Senate before beginning hearings on this matter.

I would like to thank the various tanker officers associations for writing me in this regard and informing me of their support of this legislation. Although there are many questions left to be answered concerning this problem, it does appear to be the type of legislation which would benefit the U. S.-flag merchant fleet.

>Sincerely,
>
>LEONOR K. SULLIVAN
>*Chairman*
>Committee on Merchant Marine and Fisheries
>U. S. House of Representatives

A further encouraging note was a subsequent letter from Mrs. Sullivan in which she enclosed the Bill which she had introduced together with others seeking to achieve the same goal.

>July 12, 1973
>
>This is in reply to your letter of July 10, 1973 again concerning legislation to require that a percentage of U. S. oil imports be carried on U. S.-flag vessels.
>
>In accordance with your request, you will find attached a copy of H.R. 8193, the percentage oil import bill, which I introduced together with a number of co-sponsors from the House Committee on Merchant Marine and Fisheries. This is indeed a controversial and difficult piece of legislation but I agree with you that a moderate approach is undoubtedly the best path to successful enactment of a responsive piece of legislation. As you are probably aware, the Administration in its last energy proclamation, whether or not it was inadvertent, provided for cargo preference for oil products coming into the country from the Virgin Islands. I am hopeful that the Administration can be prevailed upon to extend this principle beyond the importation of oil products from the Virgin Islands so that legislation would not even be necessary. I am meeting with the Assistant Secretary of Commerce for Maritime Affairs in the near future and I intend discussing this matter with him.
>
>Sincerely,
>
>LEONOR K. SULLIVAN
>*Chairman*
>Committee on Merchant Marine and Fisheries
>U. S. House of Representatives

While it is too early to predict the final outcome of these efforts, in the light of the current energy crisis plus the balance-of-payments situation and finally the continued political instability that prevails in the Middle East, more stress is being placed on the need for the United States to be more self-sufficient both in energy sources and in the ability to transport energy from any part of the world.

The present acute energy crisis points up sharply the need for looking at every facet in respect to solving it or at least ameliorating it—new sources of energy, more efficient use of energy, and a more realistic look at our relations with oil-producing countries. In respect to new sources of energy such as coal, oil-tar sands, solar energy, and nuclear fuels, these are all possibilities but not near-term solutions. Even if the United States could become self-sufficient for its energy needs this could become prohibitively expensive and could have economic backlash effects—slowing down and/or eliminating certain industrial activities which are the bulwark of the United States economy. More efficient use of energy will be a *must* for the future and already is proving of value. But it would be wishful thinking to believe that, at the rate energy requirements are increasing each year, even with the most efficient use of energy there still would not be a serious short-fall.

This brings us to the approach which promises both immediate amelioration and long-range reasonable adjustments. Oil-producing nations—and their number is increasing—are just as interested in improving their standard of living as we are. The forces of competition will establish the fact that no nation nor any small group of nations can forever or even for a prolonged period embargo a product as necessary to the world economy as is petroleum. There may have to be some political input by the United States to provide a better climate for relations among nations currently in conflict and to advise oil-producing nations that it is not in their best interests, even economically, to deny to the rest of the world the opportunity to engage in fair-trade relations.

Since petroleum for the foreseeable future will be obtained from sources far removed from the consuming centers of the United States—and Alaska can be included in these far-removed sources—there will be a continued need for tankers. It is urgent therefore that encouragement in both the building and the operating of American-flag vessels be provided by Congress and the Maritime Administration. At this moment it would appear that the quickest and least expensive route is the subsidy route. And if some accommodation can be made for major American oil companies to participate in an active building and operating program, the future can be a lot brighter for all hands.

NOTES

1. U. S. Maritime Administration, *Official Statistics 1963*.
2. Testimony, John J. Collins—Merchant Marine and Fisheries Committee,

(H.R. 1897). A bill to provide for compulsory arbitration, May 21, 1963.

3. *Journal of Commerce,* New York, July 14, 1961.

4. Boleslaw Adam Boczek, *Flags of Convenience* (Cambridge: Harvard University Press, 1962), pp. 197–208.

5. John F. Kennedy, Press Conference, June 25, 1961, Washington, D.C.

6. Independent Tanker Associations, *A Petition to Congress* (New York, March 1954), p. 16.

7. *Hearings,* U. S. Senate Sub-Committee on Merchant Marine and Fisheries of the Committee on Interstate and Foreign Commerce, Washington, April 9, 1957 (Government Printing Office, 1957), p. 170.

8. *Official Records,* JSTOA, TTOA, MTOA, GTOA, DOA, ATOA, New York.

9. Edward B. Shils, "Flags of Necessity, Flags of Convenience, or Runaway Ships?" *Labor Law Journal* (December 1962), 1025, 1026.

10. Letter, to President Kennedy from Independent Tanker Associations, May 8, 1961.

11. Letter, to Independent Tanker Associations from Frank L. Barton, Acting Under-Secretary for Transportation, May 23, 1961.

12. Letter to President Nixon from Independent Tanker Associations, June 5, 1972.

13. Letter to Rawleigh Warner, Jr., Chairman of the Board, Mobil Oil Corporation, from MTOA, July 6, 1972.

14. Letter from Rawleigh Warner, Jr., Chairman of the Board, Mobil Oil Corporation, to MTOA, July 14, 1972.

15. Testimony, Rawleigh Warner, Jr., Chairman of the Board, Mobil Oil Corporation on H.R. 13324—Maritime Subsidy Authorization Bill.

16. Conversations, Author and Henry Luck, General Manager, Marine Department, Mobil Oil Corporation, July 1972.

17. *NAM Reports,* June 11, 1973, National Association of Manufacturers, New York.

18. Letter, to Author from Exxon Company, U.S.A., December 4, 1973, attached document entitled "Cargo Preference Issue."

19. *Ibid.*

20. *Ibid.*

21. *Ibid.*

22. Thomas C. Barger, "Middle Eastern Oil Since the Second World War," *Annals,* American Academy of Political and Social Science (May 1972).

11

Differences Between 'Independents' and 'Nationals'

IT MAY BE COMFORTING FOR SOME to know that national unions have had their problems—and that their troubles have not all been with management. Jurisdictional disputes have plagued craft unions, and deep ideological differences still separate major groups within the merged AFL-CIO. Both independent unions and national unions are interested in the economic betterment of the individuals they represent. Independent unions do not have a corner on the formula to achieve this economic betterment, although their approach is calculated to achieve their objective with less friction. Therefore, to avoid seeming too idealistic or being too unrealistic in identifying the independent union with perfect harmony in employer-employee relations, when all the rhetoric has been expended against the "soulless corporation," even the most anti-employer union recognizes that the company must be economically viable if the union is going to provide its members with the various improvements they seek. Put differently: no union, militant or otherwise, wants to kill the goose that lays the golden egg—*unless* complete dedication to the Marxist concept of class conflict is the motivating force behind the union.

Certainly no leader of the AFL–CIO ever has proclaimed his objective to be the destruction of the profit system. And this posture has been consistently maintained from the founder of the AFL (Samuel Gompers) to the present leader of the combined AFL–CIO (George Meany). AFL–CIO officials regularly stress as their economic goal "more"; and the "more" they desire is obtained via collective bargaining. In other words, traditional AFL–CIO unions operate in the mainstream of the American economy—at least as far as the philosophy of free enterprise is concerned. They accept the system—even though at times to secure the "more" they may seriously disrupt that system. This is why students of AFL–CIO unions have argued successfully that ideologies—be they fascism, communism, or other totalitarian schemes—are alien to these unions and are considered more of an enemy than the most intractable employer.

To return to the difference between an independent union and the national union, it would appear that since both embrace the profit system, the difference between them is one only of *degree* rather than of *kind*. But is this true? Here perhaps is where economic power, its availability and its use, must be examined. But the more we examine it, the more we find disagreement among economists as to the ultimate good that is achieved by the indiscriminate use of power where a strong labor union is pitted against an equally strong or a not-so-strong employer. In the latter case the *immediate* goals of the labor union—increased wages and restrictive work rules—will be won. Whether those gains will adversely affect current employees (through "reduction in force" and increased automation) or reduce employment opportunities for prospective employees, cannot be documented in each case. However, in order to survive, the company must make certain serious economic adjustments and these could include taking some of the above actions.

Where the labor union is strong and the employer is equally strong, a conflict generally takes place. Based on the history of such conflicts—or strikes, as they are more properly called—there is a consequent tremendous loss in wages to employees and often a sharp curtailment of production by the company, to say nothing of the inconvenience to the public. That certain deleterious effects on other employer–employee groups whose operations are related to the company on strike occur is a further concomitant of a serious and lengthy labor dispute.

If AFL–CIO unions disrupt production, are they good or are they even necessary—and should they be tolerated? The answer in part is that, as a rule, they do not deliberately disrupt production, but rather use this economic weapon when other approaches have failed. Most unions came into existence to correct injustices in wages, in hours, in working conditions, or in all three. Without AFL–CIO unions there would be far more inequity than there is today in employer–employee relations. Finally, by the passage of such laws as the Norris-LaGuardia Act (1932), the Wagner Act (1935) and its modification, the Taft-Hartley Act (1947), labor unions today are not only tolerated but encouraged. Yet there are approaches other than national unions to solving employees' problems, and employees themselves generally are good judges as to what approach best suits their needs.

Perhaps the surest barometer of employees' wishes with regard to the kind of organization they believe will meet their requirements is to be found in the results of collective-bargaining-representation elections conducted by the National Labor Relations Board. These elections are for the sole purpose of giving employees an opportunity, by secret ballot, to designate their choice of a bargaining representative. The bargaining agent chosen must, by law, represent *all* the employees in the particular appropriate unit in subsequent dealings with the employer. In most instances these elections are the only ones ever held for this purpose. Their significance therefore is substantial.

During the period 1946 through 1970, independent unions have participated in 17,127 elections conducted by the National Labor Relations Board (NLRB).[1] Some of these elections have involved independent unions versus no union; others have pitted independent unions against AFL affiliates or CIO affiliates; or after the merger, against AFL–CIO affiliates. The Teamsters Union no longer is in the AFL–CIO federation. Therefore, they have been listed in the annual reports of the NLRB simply as "Teamsters." There have been a number of elections between independent unions and the Teamsters.

In short, independent unions have been on the battlefield of the ballot box against various other organizations and against the option of no organization, where employees have had an opportunity to make a choice. In the 17,127 elections in which they have participated, they have won more than 50 per cent.[2] Tables prepared by the election-analysis section of the NLRB as part of its annual reports give some idea of what success independent unions have had in elections conducted by that Board.

In the year 1970 independent unions won 56.2% of the elections in which they participated.[3] In elections where the opponent was a Teamster Union, they won 22 of 37 elections.[4] In contests where AFL–CIO unions were the opponents they won 47 out of 90.[5] The record therefore would appear clear that independent unions, wherever they may be and for whatever reason they may have been formed, have had a better-than-average record when participating in NLRB-conducted elections when their opponents have been national unions.

Once a union has been chosen, what has been its role in resolving employer–employee conflicts? Has it muted them or has it exacerbated them? And what long-range benefits have accompanied the use of the strike? We are not talking merely about the "right to strike." This is implicit in the right to organize which is a natural right. We are referring rather to the frequent use of the strike.

Since labor relations is not an exact science, it is next to impossible to speak definitively when discussing the total effect of work stoppages on a particular company, or even the effect of the existence of unionism itself. There are so many variables involved that no serious student of the economics of labor relations has yet attempted to predict the total outcome of the pressures brought to bear on an employer by a powerful union.

In 1966 the Special Studies Project of the Rockefeller Brothers Fund requested Derek Bok (former Dean of Harvard Law School and currently President of Harvard University) and John Dunlop* (former professor of Labor Economics at Harvard's Graduate School of Business, now Dean of Harvard College) to undertake a study of Labor and the American Community. They accepted the request and produced a most readable "tour de force." In *Labor and the American Community* Bok and Dunlop confess:

> It is also impossible to take a non-union enterprise or economy and introduce the complex institutions of collective bargaining, leaving everything else the same, and then measure the independent effects of unionization. Widespread changes typically take place in management and supervision, internal communications, the quality and morale of the work force, systems of promotion and wage payment, and the response of management through product lines, location and production methods. Collective bargaining also affects the surrounding product and labor markets. When all the factors that affect wages are so interdependent the separate influence of unionization is not readily identified.[6]

In the area of inflation and how it is affected by collective bargaining Bok and Dunlop argue:

> It is not possible, as in experimental sciences, to eliminate collective bargaining from an economy and then observe the course of wages and prices. It is necessary to thread one's way through diverse sets of indirect evidence in order to reach any judgment

---

* Dunlop was appointed Chairman of the Cost of Living Council by President Nixon on January 11, 1973 to monitor Phase III of the President's effort to control inflation.

at all on the subject.... The comparative increases in hourly earnings among different industries in the years 1960–67 should make one pause before dispersing easy generalizations about the consequences of collective bargaining on wages. The largely unorganized industries of agriculture, services and retail trade showed much larger increases than the more highly organized manufacturing sector. The increases in agriculture and retail trade were 37 and 32 per cent, respectively, as compared to 25 per cent in manufacturing. Although wage gains in unionized sectors may have had some indirect influence, the increases among the unorganized seem to have resulted much more from the tightening of labor markets independent of collective bargaining.[7]

Shades of Adam Smith, is laissez-faire alive and well?

What is especially interesting in Bok and Dunlop's study is their criticism of the administration of unions—meaning, of course, AFL–CIO national unions. The criticism is precise, friendly, and intended to be helpful. One receives two impressions from the criticism. First, that the present computerized milieu in which business organizations participate so thoroughly should be pursued by labor unions in all facets of their internal organization. Second, that national unions must provide, through education and training, for future leaders who will be able not only to hold their own with the most sophisticated management bargainer but to strengthen the structure of the union and participate in discussion and action in public policy matters.

These authors constantly emphasize the merits of giving more power, at least in these areas, to the international leadership. Their suggestions, or criticisms, imply that national unions, strongly centralized and with sufficient power at the top, are the most suitable to meet the problem of an expanding economy and especially to deal with the growth of conglomerates and multi-national companies. They also indicate a certain impatience with some of the purposes of the Landrum-Griffin Act, which was passed by Congress after the McClellan hearings and intended to ensure greater financial responsibility by unions and more effective control by the rank-and-file members. Here is what Bok and Dunlop say on the subject:

> The political process, however, interferes with administration on several fronts: It diverts the energies of leaders, *weakens* their control over subordinates particularly at the local level, interrupts continuity in office and may impede the leadership in such important tasks as raising dues to finance the organization. In addition

the political process leaves its mark on the selection and development of leaders. It greatly *limits* the opportunity for attracting leadership from outside the organization and allows the administration virtually no opportunity *to influence the composition of the pool of local officials from which higher leaders must be drawn.*[8]

This plea for elitism and strong central control by the upper echelons of national unions over their locals is not unusual among many students of the American labor movement. It parallels a plea for a stronger and more centralized government in the national political arena.

The National Maritime Union (AFL–CIO) attempted "to influence the composition of the pool of local officials from which higher leaders must be drawn" by certain revisions in their constitution.[9] Joe Curran had been president of the NMU since its inception in 1936. He also was a member of the top level AFL–CIO council. He retired in June 1973. When a slate of candidates opposed to the Curran group sought election to the national offices in 1966 they were not permitted to run by the rules of the amended NMU constitution.

The opposition leader, James Morrisey, brought the matter to the attention of the Secretary of Labor, Willard Wirtz, following the procedures outlined in the Landrum-Griffin Act. The complaint was resolved in Morrisey's favor by Justice Constance Baker Motley in the U. S. District Court for the Southern District of New York.[10] Justice Motley ruled that part of the NMU constitution with respect to "prior office holding" was in violation of the Landrum-Griffin Act, and that, therefore, the 1966 election of officers was invalid.[11]

Emphasizing that "the overriding purpose of the Labor Management Reporting and Disclosure Act [Landrum-Griffin] was to insure members of unions their right of self-government . . . the heart of union democracy," Justice Motley held that the NMU constitution as amended, "unreasonably restricted the right of members to become candidates for national office." [12] Less than one per cent of the membership met the NMU constitution's "prior office holding" requirements in the 1966 election of national officers.[13]

Clearly the Landrum-Griffin Act is intended *to protect* the rights of union members from such exclusionary tactics. But Bok and Dunlop, in principle at least, consider such a rule as impeding the choice of local officials[14] and they appear to be undisturbed by Lord Acton's maxim, "All power corrupts; absolute power corrupts absolutely."

Independent unions, which engage almost exclusively in local-level bargaining, are by their very nature "protected" from the opportunity—because it is denied to them—of becoming citadels of power. For them the union is a means to an end—improved wages and working conditions—not an end in itself. Struggles for power would be paradoxical since bargaining and all other aspects of their organization are at the local level. Rather, independent unions are the immediate tools of the trade—the trade of bargaining; and because of their limitations in the area of economic and political power they rely on the "art" of bargaining. They must be able to discern areas where their arguments can be telling, and where there are real possibilities for success, without dispersing their fire on meaningless or impossible targets. Above all, the ones who do the bargaining as a rule are well schooled in the details of their particular employment picture, so that management generally becomes respectful and impressed with them as bargainers. Most of the bargaining done by independent unions is done by employees who have been elected by their fellow-employees for this purpose. A high degree of formal education is not necessary—but integrity and honest indignation at what may appear to be inequities in the employment situation are *musts*. When all these are combined, and especially where the bargaining committee is both patient and persistent, satisfactory agreements result.

More than thirty-five years of participation in local-level bargaining have given the author the unique opportunity as an "observer participant" to see these employee representatives in action. And it has been a rewarding experience. Here the organic relationship between the employee representatives and their employer could be witnessed at work. Neither side referred to this organic relationship and both probably would have appeared puzzled at the mere mention of it. But the fact is, it was there, as it must be, because of the shared goals of these two groups.

Thus again philosophically, the independent union must be cast from a different mold than the national union. The latter has allegiance to that real but nevertheless amorphous entity called the "labor movement." In contrast, employees bargaining through an independent union are working within a framework of which they are an integral part. This is their primary purpose and here is their allegiance. And this manifests itself in countless ways, both at, and away from, the bargaining table—because whether "at" or "away from" they continue to be employees, and the organization which they created and which they maintain is as important a part of the whole as is the management or the stockholder group. Further binding them together is the fact that the members of the independent union and members of management are in most instances also members of the stockholder group. This phenomenon has not been correctly assessed or understood by most economists, because they either do not have the capacity to discern its uniqueness or, environmentally, they have been exposed to propaganda which is predicated on the assumption that the interests of "labor" are advanced by Big Labor and by Big Labor alone. There is no gainsaying that the presumed political clout of Big Labor impresses many economists—and even some lawmakers.

Employees who form an independent union do so either because of unsatisfactory experience with national unions or from an intuitive belief that their employment relation will be more suitably served by an organization which confines its membership and its bargaining to the employees of one company. Based on the writer's knowledge of the beginnings and workings of these organizations, it may be asserted that the independent union considers itself an integral part of the company in the sense that the employees of the company and the individuals for whom the "independent" bargain collectively are the same people.

Except for economic arguments to support its position in bargaining, the "independent" does not look beyond the framework of the immediate employer–employee relationship of the particular company. This, however, hardly is the relationship of national affiliated unions to employers with whom they bargain; such a nonadversary posture would be incongruent with their belief in the "solidarity of labor."

Employees do not generally inquire into the philosophic roots of the independent union. It is the tool they believe necessary to pry loose certain economic advantages that might either be denied them or be slow in coming. Captain Victor Lee, a long-time member of the JSTOA and elected to its executive committee, expressed it in the following letter written in November 1972. It reflects the nostalgia that comes naturally to all retirees:

> As I sit in my sun porch looking out at the bare trees on this blustery November day, my thoughts drift back to the year 1938 when I was serving as Second Mate on the s.s. *E. M. Clark*.

Captain Andrew B. Jakobsen came aboard and started recruiting officers for a new independent association to be called Jersey Standard Tanker Officers Association. At that time I was a member of the Masters Mates & Pilots Union which did nothing for me but collect dues.

Captain Jakobsen explained how the JSTOA would work—it was being created in order to improve conditions in general for the officers of the Standard Shipping Company fleet. What I particularly liked about it was that all the officials of the association would be active sea-going officers. If my memory serves me correctly dues were one dollar a month. Through the years we've made great gains such as seniority pay, higher wages with side benefits, and a major breakthrough in paid leave. Formerly throughout the maritime industry thirty days' paid leave was granted after twelve months of service. It then progressed, through efforts of our association, to ninety days' work and thirty days off, later improved to eighty days on and forty days off. This was far in excess of what the national unions were able to achieve and we did not lose a single day's pay in the interim.

Oh, yes, I recall we had some very tough bargaining sessions, but logic and common sense always prevailed. I remember that after each new contract was signed a feeling of good will and respect existed on both sides. My long years of service as an Executive Committee member have convinced me that an independent union in the marine field is the answer to the national maritime unions' strike-prone policy of the "sledge hammer"!

In closing I feel secure in the knowledge that our officers will see the wisdom of continuing independence from all outside temptations.[15]

Social scientists in the late-nineteenth century talked in Darwinian terms of "survival of the fittest" to explain in part man's ruthlessness vis-à-vis his fellow man, especially in the area of economics. Perhaps "quest for power" is the most appropriate expression to generalize man's passion and pride in pursuing his objective.

Cardinal Newman's celebrated *The Idea of a University* represents an effort to put in proper perspective the role of the university in forming for man a habit of mind which would last him through his lifetime. But Newman never claimed that a liberal discipline despite its attributes of freedom, moderation, and wisdom could directly instill virtue: "Quarry the granite rock with razors, or moor the vessel with a thread of silk; then you may hope with such keen and delicate instruments as human knowledge and human reason, to contend against those giants, the passion and pride of man."[16] These "giants" cast their shadow over all bargaining.

It is a never-ending struggle. On the one hand there is the impatient employee who wants everything someone else has, and immediately, with no thought of whether or not this is in his own long-range interest; on the other hand there are short-sighted managements who to save a dollar today will unwittingly hasten their employees into the waiting embrace of some giant union. And when this happens they rationalize their action by arguing that now the company is competitive; that wages, overtime rates, vacations, and fringes have as a result become uniform in the industry. Greater stability in labor relations will, these company labor-relations experts confidently assure their top echelon, be an added dividend to their presumed improved competitive position.

Where corporate top management accepts this kind of rationalization from its employee-relations people there is a clear lack of wisdom and vision; they have caused the demise of an instrument of stability and harmony. Its loss will, in the long run, be a disservice to the corporation.

For this type of middle (and in this instance also mediocre) management, it is just too much trouble to listen patiently and with consideration to the just demands and complaints of the employees voiced by their elected representatives. It means nothing to many in middle management that their abrasiveness and displays of annoyance and irritation with the impassioned and lengthy arguments of the independent union leadership on occasion drive some despairing and disillusioned leaders to see what they believe is "power" or "muscle" elsewhere.

A few in middle management believe that *who* they deal with is a matter of the "mechanics of bargaining." As far as they are concerned their job as bargainer is intact. As a matter of fact their stature, they believe, could be enhanced. Dealing with big unions means that the stakes are higher, the threat of work stoppages is greater, and the potential economic harm to the company extremely likely. When and if a settlement is reached, therefore, it could become a big feather in their ever enlarging hat.

But what damage is done by their short-sightedness! The loss of whatever loyalty to, and identity with, the company that could have been cultivated cannot be retrieved. No longer do they have employees highly motivated to work together toward a common goal. Instead there is an alien protagonist whose sole reason for existence is to perpetuate a militancy which at best makes the company less competitive or encourages it to pass on its negotiated gains as a cost to the consumer; and, at worst, disrupts the even flow of goods and services, thereby damaging all members of the company—stockholders, management, and employees—while leaving the public helpless. Meanwhile, this fortunately small segment of middle management merrily goes along. There is a diabolical art in creating a fire and then being the fastest fireman to the scene. And while this is going on some ostrich-like top-management people act like Nero while Rome burns.

The tragic part of such short-sightedness—where it exists—is that there are large issues facing the American system of free enterprise today, and it needs all the cohesiveness and moral stature it can muster to meet them. First among these issues is a growing skepticism toward the system itself. The old opponents, Socialists and other Marxist groups, laboriously continue to offer their brand of the "good society." But based on its demonstrated bankruptcy where it has been tried, in Soviet Russia and her satellites, East Germany, Poland, and similarly oriented states, it hardly can be said to have hastened a higher standard of living for the average individual. Otherwise it would not have been necessary to build a wall to keep East Germans from seeking greener economic pastures in West Germany—to say nothing of the opportunity such escape offered, to be a free person in every respect.

The new menace to our free society is the alleged large group of "turned off" members of the middle class, who claim to be embarrassed by the richness of America's material prosperity and who are a self-constituted New Class practicing a New Politics. Comprised for the most part of the later crop of the college-educated middle class, they are endeavoring to separate themselves from the commercial and industrial middle class (from which they spring) by embracing with "passion and pride" a disdain for anything which, they claim, contributes to the pollution of our environment. And this includes an unwillingness to work in the economic system—a system which, even with its faults, has made the life of the average American from the cradle to the grave (using the standard of living as a measure) the highest ever achieved in the world for so large a group. But facts such as these do not discourage the New Class. And since there always is something to distress us, the New Class will feed on this distress—although their remedies for it are remote and unreal. Those close to this new phenomenon (which sometimes calls itself a "conscience constituency"), such as *Commentary* editor Norman Podhoretz, see it as an undisguised desire for power. He calls it a sort of "liberal putschism." [17] Irving Kristol, one of the brighter lights in political and social analysis, sums up their goal: "The simple truth is that the professional classes [the new-breed lawyers, doctors, teachers, etc.] of our modern bureaucratized societies are engaged in a class struggle with the business community for status and *power*." [18] Where this struggle will end no one can foretell. But the New Class could grow substantially by catching the winds of discontent among some consumer groups, and well-intentioned conservationists. They could especially gain in numbers by a rapprochement with Big Labor or some segments of it.

Recent bestsellers such as Charles Reich's *The Greening of America* are built on disenchantment with the American system of free enterprise. Like all generalizations, they contain classic examples of woeful corporate conduct, which then are enlarged to become the whole story. In addition, scores of articles with a similar viewpoint appear in magazines and the daily press with such negative but attention-catching titles as "Can a Worker Find Happiness in a Dull Job?" All these prophets of doom share one thing in common—a desire, conscious or otherwise, to cripple the concept of optimism, so long identified with the American dream.

Ultimate and complete happiness is not to be found on this earth —through wealth, fame, or even power. But there can be happiness here, and one should never be reconciled to injustices and the other ills which plague society. Tools can be fashioned to make some progress toward eliminating these ills. It is a disservice, however, to entice society with romantic visions of the millennium, while convulsively tearing up the roots of that part of the past which has proved itself.

No one disputes the fact that where a national union wins a Labor Board election it can begin to bargain for the employees in that appropriate unit with considerably more economic force than can the independent union. This economic force must, of course, in the final analysis come from the employees themselves. They are the ones who must do the striking and the picketing. National unions can muster that force—i.e., the strike, the picket line, and the like —because they can call upon other locals within their national union for assistance, or by virtue of their size can single out a particular employer and attempt to make him comply with their demands. The Teamsters Union is a classic example of this approach.

Where the opponents—the employer and strong national unions —are evenly matched, the result many times is a long-drawn-out strike or else, as has happened, agreement is reached without economic war. On occasion some of these agreements have been termed "sweetheart" agreements: where the union obtains less than it should for its members in exchange for some alleged advantage to the union; on a lower moral plane a "sweetheart" agreement represents a personal benefit to the union leadership. "Sweetheart" agreements are indefensible and where documented (which is difficult to do) cause union leadership serious trouble. The more usual agreement between a strong union and a strong company or industry where there is no economic warfare sometimes is called a cost-push agreement. Such agreements, many economists argue, penalize the public with sharply higher prices. Other economists maintain that these agreements ultimately affect employees adversely through such moves as a reduction in force, which the company makes to meet the cost of the "package." There are so many ramifications and differences of opinion among economists and others as to the effect on certain segments of the economy of the bargaining of extremely strong unions that to attempt to provide answers would be simplistic in the extreme.

However, when the powerful International Ladies Garment Workers Union (ILGWU) recently appealed to Congress for protective tariffs to stop the inroads being made by the Japanese, among others, they emphasized that jobs of Americans were being lost because of the sharp disparity in wage rates between American and Japanese workers. Where the blame lies—if blame is the word —can be argued ad infinitum. Even Leonard Woodcock, President of the United Automobile Workers, and known, as had been Walter Reuther, for his wide-ranging international free-trade views, complained recently about competition from foreign-made cars. Woodcock would like to see foreign cars manufactured in the United States.[19] At the moment this is wishful thinking, at least on a large scale.

Certain employers are quick to accuse unions of pricing themselves out of the market. But such pronouncements are understandably propagandistic when issued by an employer who in the heat of an economic battle with a union is making an indirect appeal to his employees by raising the specter of unemployment. Union propaganda machines rush to their mimeographs, or employ newspaper ads, to condemn such fear tactics. Nevertheless, *jobs are being lost,* as was pointed out by Louis Stulberg, President of the ILGWU, at a news conference held on the day the ILGWU staged a nationwide demonstration to dramatize the growing strength of the Rising Sun, among others, and its effect on imported women's apparel. Stulberg stated that, in the mid-1950s, 4 per cent of the clothing that Americans bought came from abroad. By 1971, he said that as a result of imported goods from Japan, Hong Kong, and other low-wage countries, such purchases had risen to 25 per cent.[20]

The immediate advantage of a wage gain to an individual employee does not cause him to be concerned about its possible effect on overall employment. Should that wage gain, or any other economic benefit, not be able to be absorbed by the enterprise and have the firm continue competitive, the company would have difficulty demonstrating this to the average employee. It would be too much to ask individual employees to program the cost of their wage- and fringe-benefit increases to determine their total economic impact. And even if they could know the impact, they simply would shrug their shoulders and deem it inexorable. No man is a philosopher when it comes to his own paycheck, unless his philosophy be that of pragmatism.

Although independent unions have more than held their own in the total economic gains secured for those whom they represent, at least in the maritime and steel industries, it is a fact that rarely have they taken to the streets to achieve these gains. Again we must return to the basic philosophic difference—which implicitly involves the tactics used—between the independent union and the national union, to learn how these gains were made *without the use of economic force*. A partial answer lies in the economy itself, the supply–demand situation, and the necessity for an employer who wishes to recruit and retain good employees to pay at least prevailing wages and meet prevailing practices. Then why are work stoppages, associated with national unions, necessary? A quick though not complete reply is that many of them are not necessary. Some stoppages involve union rivalry; some are sheer expressions of power; still others result from mistakes by union officials or restlessness among the rank and file or maybe a tactic to make a breakthrough, to achieve a pattern decided by the high command. Sometimes in a major industry where the national union leadership has set its sights on certain economic goals, one company may become the target to test the feasibility of reaching them. There always will be economic warfare of one sort or another, even as unfortunately there always will be military conflict. Man is competitive by nature and the will to win all is not often slowed.

Compromise is considered by some as tantamount to capitulation. Woe to the leader of the national union who cautions delay when the crowd is roaring for blood—even though his earlier demagoguery might have stimulated their bloodlust. Nor is the company without blame if they follow an "all win" policy and deliberately bait the union in order to square some previous victory by the union. There is little middle ground for the necessary maneuvering that must be done by both sides, if each side considers the other an implacable enemy. But rule or ruin seems to be in vogue in the relations between some trade unions and some managements, and unfortunately in other segments of society as well. Solzhenitsyn in a broader context summed it up in his Nobel Prize lecture.

> Our twentieth century has turned out to be crueler than those that went before it, nor did everything horrible in it end with its first half. Those very same caveman emotions—greed, envy, unrestraint, mutual hatred—which, as they moved, assumed such high-sounding pseudonyms as class, race, mass, or *trade union struggle,* are tearing our world apart and reducing it to chaos. Caveman unwillingness to accept compromises has been elevated into a theoretical principle and is considered to be a virtue of orthodoxy. It requires millions of victims in endless civil wars. It keeps drumming into our hearts that there are no stable and universal concepts of justice and good, that all values are fluid, that they change, and that this means one must always act as suits one's party. Any professional group, as soon as it finds a convenient moment TO GRAB SOMETHING OFF, even if it has not been earned, even if it is unneeded, will right away grab it off, and society can go fall apart. The upward and downward oscillations of Western society, as seen from outside, are approaching at both extremes that point where the entire system will be unable to return to a state of stability and must fall into ruin. Violence, continually less restrained by the confines of a legality established over the course of many generations, strides brazenly and victoriously through the whole world, unconcerned with the fact that its sterility has already been manifested and proven many times in history. Nor is it merely brute force that triumphs but its trumpeted justification also: the whole world is being flooded with the crude conviction that force can do everything and righteousness and innocence nothing.[21]

The "high sounding pseudonyms" mentioned by Solzhenitsyn, "class, race, mass, or *trade union struggles,*" are almost totally absent from the lexicon of local-level bargaining. This does not mean that such bargaining is as smooth as a Sunday School meeting—far from it. In bargaining neither side is a choir of angels, and docility hardly is their hallmark. This is good. For were it to be otherwise the situation would be suspect. But the very limitations of independent unions in respect to the economic weapons available to them makes it all the more necessary that they pursue the "art" of bargaining patiently and with persistence. No easy path exists either for management or for the "independent" in local-level bargaining. In fact each party often has to work harder, in preparing for the bargaining as well as in the actual bargaining, than is true where national-union bargaining occurs. This phenomenon is explained by repeating that it is *employees* who are the representatives doing the local-level bargaining. They are knowledgeable and have a deep sense of obligation to their constituents—and they do not retreat readily.

In many respects it is easier to deny a demand made by a national union which by its nature is a stranger to the company than to refuse a request made by a member of the family. If the request must be rejected in the latter situation, any intelligent bargainer for management makes every effort to explain to the employee representatives why it is not feasible or economically possible *at the time* to acquiesce.

Among the hardest things for individuals to understand are the economic facts of life—if this means one does not get what one wants. No explanation, no matter how gently couched, can remove the disappointment of rejection. National unions can, if the issue is sufficiently serious, call the employees out on strike. Independent-union representatives must do what they can to salvage something from the seeming wreckage of dashed hopes and —more importantly—explain this to their constituents, even to the extent of seeking ratification of a package that falls far below what the employees expected.

It takes a lot of courage and understanding to reach a compromise on anything. In collective bargaining reaching a compromise in order to conclude an agreement is especially difficult —and delicate. Nor is it all that easy for a management which endeavors to keep the good will of its employees and to convince their representatives that they have given all they can in the light of prevailing wages and other conditions, and with an eye to the continued viability of the company—without which neither management nor the employees can survive.

That independent unions have for the most part survived these mini-crises when their accomplishments have fallen far short of their objectives is a credit to the common sense of their leadership. A recognition, even though reluctant, that one poor bargaining period does not imperil the union's future must be patiently and completely explained to the membership. Not to do this forfeits any claim to responsible leadership. Any demogogic denouncement of management—unless demonstrably deserved—represents a failure to face up to reality, and unfairly stimulates false hopes among the membership.

These then are the differences between the independent union, identified as it is with local-level bargaining, and the national union. The differences run deep because of their basically divergent philosophies how best to meet the everyday problems of the average employee.

NOTES

1. Annual Reports, Eleventh–Thirty Fifth, National Labor Relations Board, 1946–1970, United States Government Printing Office (Washington, D. C. 1946–1970).
2. *Ibid.*
3. *Op. cit.*, Thirty-Fifth Annual Report, Table 13.
4. *Ibid.*
5. *Ibid.*
6. Derek C. Bok and John T. Dunlop, *Labor and the American Community* (New York: Simon and Schuster, 1970), pp. 286, 287
7. *Ibid.*, pp. 284, 285.
8. *Ibid.*, p. 187; emphasis added.
9. National Maritime Union (AFL–CIO), *Constitution* as amended, 1963.
10. *Wirtz v. National Maritime Union of America*, 284 F.Supp. 47 (U.S. District Court, S. D. New York, 1968).
11. *Ibid.*
12. *Ibid.*
13. *Ibid.*
14. Bok and Dunlop, *Op. cit.*, pp. 90, 91.
15. Letter, Victor Lee, November 4, 1972.
16. Russell Kirk, *The Conservative Mind* (London: Faber, 1954), p. 255.
17. *Wall Street Journal*, December 21, 1972, p. 12.
18. *Ibid.*
19. *New York Times*, October 20, 1972, p. 23.
20. *New York Times*, November 17, 1972.
21. Aleksandr I. Solzhenitsyn, *The Nobel Lecture on Literature*, trans. T. P. Whitney (New York: Harper & Row, 1972), pp. 24–26; italics added.

12

Problems of Big Labor

NONE OF US CAN PREDICT THE FUTURE. Man, endowed by nature as he is with an intellect and a free will, is influenced by a variety of phenomena which range all the way from his social background to a promise or threat made in the past twenty-four hours. Some of these influences are exceedingly strong. All manner of social scientists, behavioral and otherwise, have tried to predict what man will do in a given set of circumstances or, looking backward, to explain why he acted in the manner he did. But none of these social scientists claims that he has the absolute answer to man's conduct in the sense of a proved mathematical or chemical formula. Perhaps it is the very elusiveness of man's free will that makes scientific projections regarding man's future actions as well as their explanations of his past actions so prone to error.

To postulate therefore that a certain type of organization for employees is the "best" for them is dangerous. And even if it appeared to be the best—is it best both short-range and long-range; and if it could be ascertained that it were the best, both short- and long-range, does this necessarily mean it is the best for the rest of society? Obviously the answers to all of these questions involve a judgment, and when judgments are made there will be those who disagree. And so the issue of representation comes back to the employees themselves who make pragmatic decisions based on their experience, if any, with existing labor organizations. Or perhaps their decision is based on a *belief* in the promises or the structure of a certain labor organization, which convinces the employee that this is the one most likely to fulfill his needs and desires.

Although employees are free to express their choice of organization by ballot in NLRB-conducted elections, they can be persuaded by carefully prepared propaganda to cast their vote for organizations which by their nature offer little hope of helping them to reach their short-range objectives—improved working conditions—and less hope of achieving their long-range goals, stability and continuity in their employment. While this is unfortunate, it is the price we all pay for participation in the democratic system—and we pay it willingly.

In practice, once a labor organization is chosen, whether by NLRB election or otherwise, there is a strong tendency for it to remain the collective-bargaining representative of the group that originally selected it. "Ins" are never easy to get "out" and there is no mechanism for automatic representation-elections at regular intervals as in political elections. However, under the Landrum-Griffin Act there is a requirement that the officers of a particular union must stand for election every three years, or more often if the union's constitution and by-laws so provide.[1] This affords some opportunity for change at least in the leadership, if the members desire it.

While the author believes that local-level bargaining logically is the most suitable for all concerned—employees, management, stockholders, and the general public—practically speaking, the hope at this time of any substantial increase in local-level bargaining through the medium of the unaffiliated local union is dim indeed. The reasons are many. Primary among them is that big unions are well entrenched both politically and financially. The various forms of union security, the union shop, dues check-off, payment of full wages year round to union shop committeemen in many industries such as automobile and steel, plus protection under a host of federal and state laws, and finally, union acceptance as a fait accompli by most employers, make the possibility of any substantial change remote.

On the other hand, the apparent disillusionment with national unions as reported in a recent poll conducted by Opinion Research Corporation could argue to a forthcoming upheaval in the house of labor.[2] A special report entitled "Trouble Plagues the House of Labor" in the October 28, 1972 issue of *Business Week* talks about the current, less sympathetic, feeling for the union movement as an underdog, stating "criticism of labor is, in fact, coming from all sides." [3]

Liberal intellectuals, eager for a resurgence of union militancy and radicalism, condemn many unions as ultra-conservative, even reactionary. The identification of "hard hats" with extreme patriotism is another indication of disfavor by certain union groups among unions of a "far left" persuasion. Strikes that seriously inconvenience the public—transportation stoppages, interruption and even temporary cessation of utility and other services—have turned the general public toward compulsory arbitration as a solution. Compulsory arbitration is the antithesis of free collective bargaining.

Other critics, generally from the labor intelligentsia, unhappy with what they consider the purely economic activity of big unions, recommend that they play a larger role in the political arena. For example, in a recently edited volume *American Labor: The Twentieth Century,* Paul Jacobs writes of "The Failure of Collective Bargaining." Here he charges that "labor leaders show very little concern over the weakening of the links that once held liberals and labor together." [4] Written in 1968, this charge was abundantly proved in the 1972 presidential election when George Meany put the AFL–CIO on record as refusing to endorse George McGovern, the choice of the liberal wing of the Democratic Party. Jacobs urges greater political involvement for big labor: "Now unions must move on from the simple economic level. In Israel, in the Scandinavian countries, in England and in many other foreign lands unions are an integral part of the political system, not onlookers as they are in America where the simplistic AFL tradition of rewarding friends and punishing enemies in the political arena is still dominant." [5]

Another contributor to *American Labor: The Twentieth Century* is one of the better-known labor intellectuals, who for years was Research Director of the Textile Workers Union of America (AFL–CIO)—Solomon Barkin. In an excerpt from his *Decline of the Labor Movement,* published in 1961 at the Center for the Study of Democratic Institutions, Barkin, despairing of quick acceptance by old-line labor leaders of his formula for reinvigorating the "union movement," makes a strong appeal for unions of government employees:

> The government also has a responsibility to set a model for private industry by burying its obsolete theories of sovereignty, scrapping its autocratic personnel policies and frankly accepting unionism and collective bargaining for its own employees. The new federal administration can make a major contribution by publicly endorsing unionization and collective bargaining for federal employees.[6]

Barkin's advice apparently was taken by President Kennedy who issued Executive Order No. 10988 in January 1962, authorizing collective bargaining between the various offices of the Federal

Government and unions representing these employees.[7] This spur, plus equal acquiescence in the recognition of, and bargaining with, unions by state and local governments, has resulted in the greatest increase in AFL–CIO union membership since World War II.

There have been other criticisms of American labor unions, some of it from within the highest echelons of the AFL–CIO leadership. The late Walter Reuther, long-time leader of the United Auto Workers, highlighted the dissatisfaction of many in the AFL–CIO fold in his now famous Administrative Letter of February 8, 1967 in which he listed at length the shortcomings of the AFL–CIO of which his United Auto Workers still were members. He charged the AFL–CIO with failure to meet its responsibilities and accused the leadership (the Executive Council) of "indifference . . . and policies reflecting narrow negativism."[8] Subsequently, the United Auto Workers seceded from the AFL–CIO, and to date they have not rejoined.

George Meany has not taken such criticism lightly. As a sample of his attitude toward those who question the policies, programs, or record of the AFL–CIO, Meany, in his address to the Fifth Constitutional Convention of the AFL–CIO in 1963, sought to puncture by his pungent prose all such charges; not only those then current, but he even anticipated future criticism of a similar nature, including that later made by Walter Reuther:

> We have been favored in recent years with a stream of free advice and opinion graciously extended to us by a new school of critics—sometimes termed the "disenchanted liberals" or "disillusioned friends of labor."[9]

Bok and Dunlop, in their introductory chapter "Trade Unions and Public Opinion," cite the intellectual community as disillusioned by the development of Big Labor—or, as they claim, its failure to develop in accordance with left-liberal ideals.

> Over the past thirty years, a constant critique of the labor movement has been carried on by writers of a liberal or left persuasion. Much of this work has taken the form of articles appearing in such magazines as *Progressive, Commonweal, The Nation* and *The New Republic*, as well as in such books as B. J. Widick's *Labor Today*, C. Wright Mills' *New Men of Power*, and Sidney Lens' *The Crisis of American Labor* to cite a few well known examples. These writers have not been professors specializing in labor relations, although a few, like Mills, have been academic scholars. Nor have they held influential posts in a union, although several, like Lens, have had some connection with the labor move-

ment. Yet they doubtless speak for a large segment of the liberal intellectual community, and their criticisms are already being echoed repeatedly by students associated with the "New Left." [10]

They return to this theme in their concluding chapter, where they reluctantly admit that ". . . the liberal criticisms are captured with particular vividness in the following editorial from *The New Republic*.

> As the delegates [to the AFL–CIO Convention] examined the state of their unions, they are bound to confront the fact that dedicated youngsters, who in the thirties would have been on labor's picket line, are marching to a different drummer. They are fighting elsewhere, for civil rights, peace, or better garbage collection in a slum. To them, the AFL–CIO is just another protective association, speaking for the possessors and not the dispossessed. The unions, they say, care more about repealing a section of the Taft-Hartley Act than about the poor, and more concerned with security and seniority for themselves than with a better life for all. Such criticism is too sweeping to be just. But there's no doubt about it, the drama has gone out of the labor game, and it cannot be put back by public relations.[11]

Bok and Dunlop also quote from A. H. Raskin's* article entitled "The Obsolescent Unions" which appeared in *Commentary* in July 1963: ". . . the conquest of want, illiteracy, intolerance, the building up of both health and decent housing, the realization of the Scientific Golden Age would be vastly more inspiring to union membership and leadership alike than their present ever more routine function in the policing of *day to day plant grievances* and the writing of mechanized contracts." [12] The tiring chore of policing agreements to be certain that the little things which mean so much to so many in the plant, on the assembly line, or on board ship, are taken care of, is never exciting to armchair labor-relations philosophers. Resolving a grievance is hard work, and today like other things associated with work it is taboo. It is easier for Raskin to talk in vague generalized terms of "illiteracy," "intolerance," and "mechanized contracts." [13]

Erstwhile proponents of Big Labor in intellectual circles obviously are displeased with the way their hoped-for activist arm is functioning. Given the doctrinaire stance of most intellectuals and their perennial unwillingness to come to grips with things as they are and with people as they are, they cannot reconcile their

---

* Raskin for years was Labor Editor for the *New York Times*.

hopes and their beliefs that a better world is just around the corner —if people would just follow *their* plan for the future—with the hard realities that while man does not live by bread alone he still insists on having that bread first. Some labor liberals will argue he has that bread and with plenty of butter on it now. But try telling that to the average employee who is inclined to be quite self-centered—some more than others.

Bok and Dunlop and other friends of Big Labor are concerned for its future. They see the possibility of *more* not less government control; *more* public skepticism and hostility and less looking to labor unions by the average workman as the answer to his problem.[14] The slow growth of unions between 1958 and 1970 highlights this "less looking to labor unions." According to the previously mentioned *Business Week* article, "Today's bigger trade union movement represents a declining part of the work force. Labor's share has dropped from 33.2% in 1955 to 27.4% in 1970."[15] When it is realized that the growth of unionism among public employees, federal, state, and local, including teachers, has been phenomenal during the same period, the failure of Big Labor to grow in the *private sector* becomes more significant.

To shore up the image of Big Labor with the public, Bok and Dunlop suggest greater involvement with government. They do not recommend outright that Big Labor become the basis of a political party as has been done in European countries—which in large measure accounts for the different role labor unions play in these countries—but they make oblique suggestions which, if the "mix" is right, could do just that. One of their heroes is the late Walter Reuther. Reuther's ambition always had been to make Big Labor more politically potent. Reuther argued that the logical way to do this was to have labor unions become the basis of a political party. This had been done successfully in England toward the end of the nineteenth century. Why not in the United States? One reason perhaps was the socialistic basis for all European labor parties, including the Labour Party in England. This was repugnant to the average member of American labor unions. Certainly George Meany has expressed himself unequivocally on the subject. This was one of the underlying reasons for the friction between Reuther and Meany while Reuther was a member of the AFL–CIO Executive Council. And so the ideological battle continues. The liberal intellectuals clearly are unhappy because both the top echelon of the AFL–CIO and the rank-and-file union members with few exceptions will not embrace the "planned society" in which all wrongs are righted and everyone shares the joys of Alice in wonderland—at least on paper.

In some measure this rejection of their modern millennium accounts for their derogatory remarks. But the labor liberals have not given up, and as long as Big Labor remains big, the hope of conversion will spring eternal. Meanwhile on the subject of what Big Labor can do to improve its image, Bok and Dunlop recognize and sympathize with their difficulties in seeking to correct what these two scholars see as the social ills of the day:

> One can readily sympathize with the visions of other critics who deplore the failure of union leaders to seize opportunities to turn their talents to new fields: organizing the poor, mobilizing the members to fight for consumer protection, and taking the lead in searching for a more meaningful life for workers caught between their television set and the tedium of a semi-skilled, repetitive job. In one sense, unions seem naturally suited to such tasks in view of their experience in organizing mass movements, their large membership, and their commitment to high social purposes. Yet, critics invariably overlook the enormous difficulties involved: the members' lack of interest in undertaking ventures outside the traditional union domain, their unwillingess to see their dues expended for such purposes, the shortages of talented leadership in labor's ranks and the pressures on existing leaders, whose time and energy are already stretched thin attending to conventional union tasks. In the face of such limitations, even a leader as gifted and energetic as Walter Reuther has been unable to make noteworthy progress in organizing the poor, expanding union membership, altering Detroit politics, or expanding the skilled job opportunities for Negro members. By underestimating these problems, liberal critics have succeeded—after two decades of biting prose—in accomplishing virtually nothing except to antagonize the union leadership.[16]

One needs but read the recently published biography of George Meany, president since 1952, to realize both the strength and the weaknesses of that big umbrella—the Federation (AFL-CIO)—over the many large, medium, and small autonomous unions which comprise this complex.[17] It has been damned by its critics on the left for failure to act as one monolithic group on social subjects; damned by its critics on the right for claiming to speak for all labor especially when lobbying inside and outside the halls of Congress; and damned by the public for being too big. A poll conducted by Opinion Research Corporation, a McGraw-Hill subsidiary, in 1971-72 indicated that "Public opposition to the continued growth of unions, in membership and in power, has risen. Through the 1960s the percentage of those who felt that unions are too big or are big enough fluctuated between 60% and 65%. It rose sharply to 71% over the past three years." [18]

Does all of this sound the death knell of Big Labor? Hardly. When one realizes that the annual income of the United Auto Workers is in excess of $100-million (and the Teamsters' with a larger membership and higher dues obviously tops this), it is not likely that the demise of these organizations is imminent. And so long as there are callous employers and chiseling employers—and very likely there always will be plenty of both—employees will continue to form unions or to seek membership in existing ones. It is vitally important, not just for unions, but for all the people of the United States, that employees' right to form and/or join unions of their own choosing be jealously guarded from intimidation, outright or veiled, from any source. Employers do not do their employees a service in showing a preference for one union over another when an election is being held. Employees can be told the virtues and the drawbacks of various labor organizations as the employer sees them—but he may not couch his criticism or praise in such language as could be construed by the voting employees as a promise to them or as a threat. Such action not only violates the law (Taft-Hartley) but is a gratuitous insult to the common sense and personal integrity of the average employee; and from a practical point of view, it can boomerang on the employer.

Once the union is chosen, the legal obligation of the employer to bargain with it is clear. What the employer bargains in the way of union security for the union can run the gamut from a maintenance of membership clause (which falls far short of the union shop), to a union shop, permitted to be bargained by Taft-Hartley, except in "right to work" states, all the way to a clause requiring the company to pay the full wages and related benefits to a union committeeman. This last individual does not perform any of the ordinary duties of his job as an employee. He functions full time as a representative of the union. This arrangement exists in varying respects in contracts between the United Auto Workers and the "big three" automobile manufacturers, General Motors, Ford, and Chrysler. There are approximately 2,000 such committeemen at Ford; and more at General Motors. At an average hourly rate of $5 paid for a 40-hour week, this amounts to $200 a week; times 52 weeks, times 2,000, this totals more than $20-million per year for Ford alone for its 2,000 committeemen. And overtime, if worked by the men in the group (there is one committeeman for every 250 employees in a group), also is payable to the committeeman.[19] General Motors and Chrysler have similar arrangements. These are parts of negotiated agreements. Because they have been negotiated apparently the NLRB does not consider this to be financial assistance to the United Auto Workers by the automobile companies which would violate the "company dominated union" provision of the Taft-Hartley Act. It is an interesting aspect of labor relations as practiced by Big Labor and some members of Big Business—the company pays the union representatives their regular pay 365 days a year to represent their employees *against the company*. With such financial backing by the company the union's existence is guaranteed forever.

But while the United Auto Workers seem secure at the moment by virtue of this company financial assistance, situations and union leadership can change. There *is,* for example, that embarrassing power struggle in the United Mine Workers Union which recently received so much unwanted (by Big Labor) publicity. When, according to liberal columnist Mary McGrory, "Arnold Miller, a disabled West Virginia coal miner, is risking his life to run for the presidency of the United Mine Workers of America," [20] and when the Labor Department is spending $4-million to insure that he gets an honest count, Big Labor's image is in big trouble. Under the Landrum-Griffin Act (intended to give rank-and-file members an opportunity to know more about their union and encourage greater membership participation in it), Federal Judge Charles R. Bryant, after reviewing the 1969 campaign of the incumbent president of the United Mine Workers, W. A. (Tony) Boyle, ordered a new election.[21] Among the less attractive features surrounding the previous election was the murder of Boyle's 1969 rival, Jock Yablonski, together with his wife and daughter. Their bodies were found in their home New Year's Day 1970.

In a *New York Times* article of November 26, 1972 (written prior to the rescheduled election) entitled "Tony Boyle, Arnold Miller, and the Ghost of John L. Lewis," Laurence Learner argued that the mine workers' election is a contest between new-breed unionists supported by intellectual activists outside the union's ranks and those who are the inheritors of the policies of John L. Lewis.

Lewis, the mighty spokesman for Big Labor in the 1930s, whose canonization as the first American labor saint had almost been accomplished until he turned his back on President Franklin D.

Roosevelt when Roosevelt chose to be the first three-term President of the United States, himself had structured the United Mine Workers in the tightly controlled manner which Boyle, Lewis' successor, has continued. Said Learner:

> This is a race not only between two men, two slates, but between two views on how workers in a democratic society can govern themselves. It is a race over John L. Lewis and his legacy. For forty years Lewis ruled the U.M.W. with flamboyant paternalism, with rhetoric full of fire and militancy, and a hand that struck down all who opposed him. He took away the miner's right to elect most of their district officers, and he never saw fit to return that right. In his final years, when Lewis grew so profoundly isolated from the rest of American labor, he came increasingly to see himself as the final arbiter not only of his own union but of the entire coal industry. He no longer barked his terms at the companies. He dictated what he considered to be justice to labor and industry alike. He lent money to coal companies. He bought his union a bank. He never could stand subordinates who were not cut to a size that fit comfortably into his shadow, and he chose as his successor Tony Boyle, whom he had brought to Washington in 1948 from the presidency of the Montana district. . . .

Boyle took office in 1963 and continued Lewis' dictates and policies as if they were biblical commandments.[22]

And yet during most of Lewis' years as the most powerful labor leader in the United States, criticism of him generally was joined with flowery praise for what he had done for the miners. As this is being readied for publication the results of the mine worker's election made Miller the winner over Boyle by a vote of 70,373 to 56,334.[23]

When Jock Yablonski's son was asked to compare this Labor Department-supervised election with the previous election during which his father, mother, and sister were murdered, he said it was like comparing a Soviet-run political election with one conducted in the United States.[24] But the Boyle faction is not giving up easily. A *New York Times* article on December 29, 1972 reported that the Union's Executive Board "voted to set up a financial 'watchdog' committee of pro-Boyle men to monitor expenditures of the new administration." [25] Miller, in decidedly undiplomatic language, after calling the board's actions "illegal, short-sighted and damaging to the Union," sarcastically charged, "Boyle's board members wouldn't know the meaning of union democracy if it was written on their backsides with a blowtorch."[26] This expensive experience ($4,000,000 spent by the Labor Department just for this election) to insure membership control of their union should be sufficient to convince critics of the Landrum-Griffin Act of its necessity. But brickbats, oblique and otherwise, even by scholars of the Bok and Dunlop stamp, continue to be tossed at it.

It is significant to note that high marks had been given James Hoffa, the former president of the Teamsters Union, by the liberal establishment (including the Harvard hierarchy of labor experts); but this was before he was sent to jail. Earlier in his career Hoffa had been a guest lecturer at the Harvard Business School. His strength was considered a plus by many business leaders who looked to him to maintain labor stability in the field of transportation. He did, but at a price—and a price which the late Senator Robert Kennedy when counsel to the McClellan Committee considered far too high.

The exposure of corruption in the Teamsters Union resulting from the exhaustive McClellan Committee hearings was to lead later to a charge of jury tampering by the Teamsters' leader, which, when proven, sent Hoffa to the Lewisburg, Pennsylvania, federal penitentiary for several years. Earlier, and because of the damage done to the reputation of the AFL–CIO by the McClellan hearings, George Meany persisted (against bitter opposition from members of the Executive Council) in his efforts to make Hoffa quit the presidency of the Teamsters. When Hoffa refused to budge, Meany succeeded in bringing the matter of expelling the Teamsters from the AFL–CIO to a vote at the Federation's annual convention at Atlantic City. Said Meany, "We have got to free them from this dictatorship."[27] The vote for expulsion was 10,548,598 to 2,266,497.[28] The fateful day was December 5, 1957. In his memoir, Hoffa said:

> There is a possibility that the AFL–CIO was panicked by the crescendo of criticism directed at American Labor by [Robert] Kennedy and the McClellan Committee and wished to separate itself from what was the avowed immediate target, the Teamsters. But there's also the possibility that Kennedy whispered in the ear of an influential labor leader in the hierarchy of the AFL–CIO, suggesting he would be wise, politically, to initiate and promote the movement for expulsion of the Teamsters. Some mighty large unions were not really investigated by Kennedy and that fact is surely significant.[29]

Unfortunately, stories such as those of the Teamsters and United Mine Workers unfairly smear many labor organizations where power fights among the top leaders or rank-and-file efforts to take control are frequent. Bok and Dunlop take note of the unfairness of the general castigation of unions for the failures of the few:

> Although the record in the Country compares unfavorably with that of many other nations, legal safeguards now go far to curb dishonesty and encourage democratic behavior. Probably only a tiny fraction of all union officials in America would stoop to serious abuse. The overwhelming majority of labor leaders are honest men who take seriously their obligation to represent the interests of the members who have elected them to office.[30]

The disclosures of the McClellan Committee hearings were a revelation not only to the public but also to George Meany, who declared: ". . . we thought we knew a few things about trade union corruption, but we didn't know the half of it, one-tenth of it or the one-hundredth part of it." [31] Robert F. Kennedy, whose active role as counsel to the McClellan Committee revealed many highly questionable tactics of the Teamsters Union, told the story of the committee hearings in a popular summary entitled *The Enemy Within* published in 1960.[32]

Despite the honest shock of George Meany at the revelations of corruption by some Big Labor unions, he opposed passage of the Landrum-Griffin Bill. Not because he did not want to see a crackdown on corrupt practices, but because the bill went beyond this, and in one amendment to the Senate bill, already anathema to labor, picked up "several smelly incrustations" from representative Phil Landrum, a Georgia Dixiecrat—bans on so-called "hot cargo" contracts under which union members may refuse to work with non-union material, and on organizational picketing, where a union pickets in hopes of inducing a majority of employees to sign pledge cards.[33]

Apart from the corruption cited during the McClellan hearings and the goal of the Landrum-Griffin Act to ensure honesty in the handling of union monies and guarantee greater participation by the rank and file in their organizations, Bok and Dunlop have different ideas in the conclusions contained in their chapter "Democracy, Union Government and the Interests of the Members":

> With the passage of the Landrum-Griffin Act, the issue of union democracy should move away from broad legislative reform to a host of particular questions that vary greatly from one labor or-

ganization to another. Should both the local business agent and the assistant business agent be elected, or should the latter be appointed to ensure continuity and experience? What types of decisions should be subject to ratification? Should elections be held every year or every two or three years? Should the elections occur close to contract negotiations or will this force union officials to take irresponsible positions at the bargaining table? Few of these matters are fit subjects for legislation, and most should be judged according to the special circumstances of the particular union involved.[34]

And so the problem will continue to haunt Big Labor: how to police their organizations, not only in matters of possible corruption, but in meeting the new tests of "social responsibility"—that wonderfully nebulous expression which is defined in accordance with the definer's desire. Bok and Dunlop do not like Landrum-Griffin because it circumscribes the leaders of large labor unions where they are "planning" for the future, and must of necessity have people who are on the same ideological wavelength as themselves to implement the "planning." Assuming for the moment that we accept the conclusions of Bok and Dunlop and the school of thought they represent, do we sweep the findings of the McClellan Committee under the rug and tell the rank-and-file members that corruption is only in the eye of the beholder, and, as for the direction of the union, "father knows best"?

There just is not any easy answer to this. But it should be some sort of lesson to those union leaders and armchair philosophers of the trade union movement that when you seek government help and get it in the form of the Norris-LaGuardia Act, the Wagner and Taft-Hartley Acts, you ultimately have to pay for it. The privacy which national unions guarded so zealously in the past has given way to a goldfish-bowl situation in which government believes that it has not only the right but the duty to protect those employees whose unionization they hastened. This was an inexorable development. This protection now is afforded union members to the extent that the Landrum-Griffin Act requires all unions annually to "report and disclose" their income and expenditures to the Labor Department and to supply their members with this financial report. In addition, according to the language of Landrum-Griffin, the Secretary of Labor is authorized to "supervise" certain aspects of a union's internal administration including election of union officers. And the end is not yet in sight—especially since the large national unions no longer are private organizations but quasi-public bodies whose activities can, and do, frequently disrupt the national economy.

Big Labor is on the horns of a dilemma. To cast off all government support conceivably could lose them the anchor they now have in the various forms of union security. To acquiesce in more and more government regulation and control surely would emasculate them with the inevitable corollary of the government's stepping in to fill the vacuum. Compulsory arbitration as applied to the bargaining process would accomplish this. A third possibility is a blending of labor and government, with labor playing the game of watchful waiting while enjoying their newly discovered political importance to a Republican administration.

President Nixon appears to be skirting with such a blending. His recent inordinate attachment to big-name labor leaders and his choice of a down-to-earth, experienced labor tactician, Peter Brennan, as Secretary of Labor may be the beginning of a trend in this direction. At this time, however, none of these three possibilities has sufficient support to make a prediction as to the outcome, but each certainly contains enough dynamite to rock the ideological cradle of Big Labor.

NOTES

1. Landrum-Griffin Act (Labor–Management Reporting and Disclosures Act of 1959).
2. Opinion Research Corporation, *The Labor Union Survey*, November 14–December 14, 1972 (Princeton).
3. "Trouble Plagues the House of Labor," Special Report in *Business Week*, October 28, 1972, p. 27.
4. Paul Jacobs, "The Failure of Collective Bargaining," *American Labor: The Twentieth Century*, ed. Jerold S. Auerbach (New York: Bobbs-Merrill, 1969), p. 406.
5. *Ibid.*, p. 410.
6. Solomon Barkin, "The Decline of the Labor Movement," *American Labor*, p. 417.
7. John F. Kennedy, Executive Order No. 10988, January 1962.
8. Walter Reuther, "Disagreement with the AFL–CIO," from UAW Administrative Letter of February 8, 1967, *American Labor*, pp. 432–442.
9. George Meany, "A Reply to Labor's Critics," *American Labor*, pp. 427, 428.
10. Bok and Dunlop, *Labor and the American Community*, p. 30.
11. *Ibid.*, p. 458.
12. *Ibid.*, p. 459; emphasis added.
13. *Ibid.*, p. 460.
14. *Ibid.*, pp. 478, 487.
15. "Trouble Plagues the House of Labor," p. 68.
16. Bok and Dunlop, *op. cit.*, p. 477.

17. Joseph C. Goulden, *Meany* (New York: Atheneum, 1972).
18. "Trouble Plagues the House of Labor," p. 67.
19. Agreement, United Auto Workers and Ford Motor Company, 1970.
20. *New York Post,* November 21, 1972, p. 35.
21. *Ibid.*
22. Laurence Learner, "Tony Boyle, Arnold Miller, and the Ghost of John L. Lewis," *New York Times Sunday Magazine,* November 26, 1972.
23. *New York Times,* December 17, 1972, p. 32.
24. *Ibid.*
25. *New York Times,* December 20, 1972, p. 18.
26. *Ibid.*
27. Goulden, *Meany,* p. 251.
28. *Ibid.,* p. 251.
29. *Ibid.,* p. 252.
30. Bok and Dunlop, *op. cit.,* p. 69.
31. Goulden, *Meany,* p. 298.
32. Robert F. Kennedy, *The Enemy Within* (New York: Harper & Row, 1960).
33. Goulden, *Meany,* p. 298.
34. Bok and Dunlop, *op. cit.,* p. 91.

Conclusion

PHILOSOPHERS AND POLITICAL SCIENTISTS seem to discern a common characteristic threading its way through all of man's major decisions. Some call it man's quest for power; others, man's passion and pride; and still others, man's predilection to excessive selfishness and the aggressive spirit this engenders.

The temptation to seek power is not limited to politics in the parochial sense. It can and does appear frequently in labor's fight for power. If local-level bargaining did nothing else but preserve employees from the deadening influence of being ruled by some huge monolithic organization to which they were bound by compulsory membership, as individuals are in the large national unions, in the most minute and intimate details of their every working day, it would justify itself.

That home rule—which so many talk about and intuitively support, but which is being eroded inexorably in the name of efficiency and super planning—is, when it occurs in bargaining, *local-level bargaining*. Surely it is of vital interest to management and employees alike to make this bargaining work.

Bargaining at the local level in the maritime industry has established three things: one, that certain employees freely have chosen the instrument of the independent union as the vehicle best suited to promote their overall economic interests; by choosing it they have recognized the common concern of both labor and management in the welfare and success of the company; two, that there need not be an adversary relationship, akin to class conflict, to propose, discuss, and finally to reach an agreement satisfactory to both parties; and three, that the economic benefits, if the total compensation package is considered, are superior to those negotiated by national unions—and that in the process no loss of pay has been suffered by the employees, no interruption of operations has been experienced by the company, and there has been no injury to the public.

Local-level bargaining is a proven tool in the area of employer–employee relations. By the knowledge that continuous discord can spell disaster for the institution of which both are a part, and that no difficulty is insurmountable if the effort is made to overcome it, local-level bargaining has faced up to the economic realities of the American system of free enterprise. The ratified agreements negotiated by independent unions over many years and secured without work stoppages are the irrefutable evidence that where this has been tried it has worked remarkably well. Paradoxically, the self-interest of management and employees, instead of resulting in endless impasses, has recognized that the parties bear a complementary relation to each other.

This is more readily discernible where the bargaining is done at the local level because of the proximity of both parties to the competitive climate. The force for good for all segments of society that characterizes the competitive system is ignored by those who "plan" our lives.

That the system of competition in the marketplace preserves the freedom of unions as well as of individuals is highlighted by F. A. Hayek in *The Constitution of Liberty*. Here he stresses how perilously close to emasculation national unions may be if the trend toward greater involvement by government in the economic life of the community continues at its present pace, and especially if national unions do not agree to be treated the same as other groups and individuals in society.

> Once government undertakes to determine the whole wage structure and is thereby forced to control employment and production, there will be a far greater destruction of the present powers of the unions than their submission to the rule of equal law would involve. Under such a system the unions will have only the choice between becoming the willing instrument of governmental policy and being incorporated into the machinery of government on the one hand, and being totally abolished on the other.[1]

In the light of such somber warning, the author believes that with all of its drawbacks and difficulties—both those alleged by its opponents and those observed by the writer from the vantage point of being on the inside—local-level bargaining has merit far beyond the fact of the labor stability it encourages. Philosophically, local-level bargaining is a "natural." The strength of the independent unaffiliated unions is not determined on a scale of weights and measures, but on their acceptance as the normal method of dealing collectively with employees by management within the company.

By "acceptance" is meant the necessity on the part of management to deal fairly with the independent in all areas—wages, working conditions, and grievances. Any circumvention by management, any cutting of corners, any failure to meet competitive conditions or to give a reasonable explanation why at the time this cannot be done, will expose the leadership of the "independent" to attacks both from without and from within. National unions watch for any faltering by the independent on the economic front. The noisy minority within, who never understood fully the benefit *to them* of local-level bargaining, are only too ready to claim "I told you so," whenever the leadership of the independent cannot at least match the gains of their competition. What is amazing about critics of local-level bargaining within the union is their naïveté—their simplistic belief that big unions always get what they want, when they want it, and without a struggle. Little thought is given to the fact that, not only are national unions not always successful, but when they do have to struggle it is the employees who do the struggling—or, more precisely expressed, the striking.

There is no question that to some employees there is a sort of melodrama in confronting the employer with those famous last words "No contract, no work." Undoubtedly, it has a visceral effect for some; they are taking on the giant, and they literally are going to lay him low. Well, maybe—then again, maybe not; and even where they do, can the costs be calculated? There is such a group, generally quite small, in all organizations. They need a "cause célèbre" to become vocal and gather additional adherents. It is the task of the leaders of the independent and of the management to see that no "cause célèbre" develops. This is not easy—but thirty-five years of bargaining on behalf of independent unions has convinced the author that a mixture of patience, commonsense, and consideration by both sides will avert needless confrontations which leave no avenue for escape.

In a sense, management has a greater responsibility to prevent bargaining from reaching a point of no return—and this is where consideration counts. The independent union is a representative of the employees; it is also a political animal, and it must react with some emotion in the bargaining contest in which it is engaged.

Leaders are elected, and like leaders anywhere they are expected to produce. In business when a leader does not produce he is simply replaced; and he cannot call upon anyone to bail him out—economically or emotionally. In the larger area of politics, which includes labor organizations, the leader who does not produce will be supplanted by one who *promises* to produce. Therefore, to keep his leadership, he may bring his organization (if it is a national union) to the verge of a strike, or directly on strike. Leaders of an independent union do not as a rule have these options. They may, however, in a moment of weakness, succumb to the cries of the militant minority and seek assistance through affiliation, or otherwise, of a powerful national union. Once this takes place it is difficult if not impossible for the "independent" to extricate itself. Understandably the attraction and need for power when an impasse in bargaining occurs is like a magnet. It is difficult to resist. Reason cannot be employed successfully in such an emotional climate. And while it may be easy to say that bargaining or relations with an independent union should not so deteriorate as to invite this choice, it can happen. Although it rarely occurs, leaders of independent unions can, on occasion, taste the delights of power, and desire more of it. Affiliation seems to promise this to them.

One who believes in the overall value of the independent union can only hope in these circumstances that the leadership of the independent will continue to try to resolve the problem directly with management, no matter how serious the impasse; and that management, without necessarily capitulating, will find room to maneuver and get the bargaining ship safely back on its course. Careful planning by management (including making every effort to be at least competitive) and genuine warmth extended to the leadership of the independent, plus a deeply held belief by both sides in the value of amicable relations in local-level bargaining, will preclude brinkmanship bargaining. All parties involved in employer–employee relations (including government) should concern themselves with ways and means of encouraging local-level bargaining. The importance of an updated evaluation of this form of bargaining cannot be overstated. To change the climate will be difficult since it could involve revamping labor legislation. But first there must be a deeper understanding of the philosophy of local-level bargaining by top management.

But it needs help: help first in appreciating the role it can play in stabilizing employer–employee relations in the United States; help in educating management to the legitimate part it can play in cultivating this form of bargaining, especially by showing concern for the problems the independent leadership is asked to solve by its constituents; and help by students of labor relations who, if they must denigrate local-level bargaining for whatever reasons, should equally emphasize the shortcomings of Big Labor. This they can do in a non-partisan way by pinpointing cases of corruption; questioning alignment with, or orientation toward, totalitarian ideologies, where this may exist; estimating the cost to all parties of incessant jurisdictional squabbles; illuminating the lack of democratic procedures by certain members of Big Labor except where the bright light of Landrum-Griffin is focused on them; and, finally, by statistical reference to losses suffered from strikes, in wages to employees, in earnings to the company, and to employees and employers in related industries, not to mention inconvenience to the general public and lost markets (where this occurs) to foreign competition. This equal treatment for independent unions requested of students of labor relations follows the plea of minority political parties for equal time. It is long overdue.

Even such a firm laissez-fair proponent as Hayek, after arguing the paradox of "coercive" unions functioning in a free economy, readily admits the value of what he terms non-coercive unions.

> Unions without coercive powers would probably play a useful and important role even in the process of wage determination. In the first place there is often a choice to be made between wage increases on the one hand, and on the other, alternative benefits which the employer could provide at the same cost but which he can provide only if all or most of the workers are willing to accept them in preference to additional pay. . . . The most effective way of securing consent is probably to have *the general scheme agreed to in collective negotiations in which all the different interests are represented.* Even from the employer's point of view it would be difficult to conceive of any other way of reconciling all the different considerations that in a large organization have to be taken into account in arriving at a satisfactory wage structure.[2]

Those seeking some absolutist form of solving the difficulties between employer and employees will find it only in an absolutist state; and here it hardly can be termed a "solution." The virtue of pluralism is in the freedom to choose. In a pluralistic society there is room for the national-union as well as the independent-union concept. If a fair picture is given of the pluses and minuses of both forms of organization, at least local-level bargaining will not continue to suffer at the hands of "the friends of labor."

Certainly a more promising era of labor stability can become a reality if a deeper awareness of the *good intention* of local-level bargaining existed throughout the land. Some may consider this naïveté. But it is a naïveté fortified by years of involvement in hard bargaining. It is the kind of naïveté which pursues objectives in bargaining with a belief that the other side is equally interested in reaching agreement.

Edmund Burke's sagacious observation to his fellow members of Parliament in his reasoned *Conciliation with the Colonies* sums it up best:

> *Plain good intention*, which is as easily discovered at the first view as fraud is surely detected at last, is, let me say, of no mean force in the government of mankind.[3]

The collective bargaining process can be considered a form of government in the area of employer–employee relations.

This author believes firmly in the value of "plain good intention," where this is expressed and implemented by management and labor.

NOTES

1. F. A. Hayek, *The Constitution of Liberty* (Chicago: University of Chicago Press, 1960), p. 283.
2. *Ibid.*, p. 276; emphasis added.
3. *Burke's Politics,* edd. Hoffman and Levack, p. 64.

Index

AFL, 2–4
AFL–CIO, 4, 150–152, 169–171, 173, 177
Alaskan pipeline, 142
American Academy of Political and Social Science, 144
American Arbitration Association, 34, 78, 92, 94
American Licensed Officers Association, 84
American Merchant Marine, Economic Survey, 13–14
American Petroleum Institute, 143
American Tanker Officers Association, 105–106
American Trading and Production, 45–46, 105
Andreae, Joseph, 66–67
Arabian American Oil Company, 144
Armco, 12, 18–20, 22

Barbash, Jack, 24
Barger, Thomas C., 144
Barkin, Solomon, 169
Bentley, Helen, 13
Bok, Derek, 153–155, 170–173, 177–179
Boyle, W. A. (Tony), 175–176
Brennan, Peter, 1, 180
Bridgeo, R., 83
Brod, Robert S., 10
Bureau of Labor Statistics, 24
Burke, Edmund, 1, 80–81, 188
Business Week, 168, 172

Christensen, Bertram, 131
CIO, 4
Cities Service, 30, 41–42, 76–79, 82
Coast Guard, 55–56, 83, 89–90, 93, 115–117, 127
Colonial Pipe Line, 35, 136
Company-dominated union, 2–3, 175
Compulsory arbitration, 133–135, 169, 180
Crowley, Francis, 83

Deepwater Officers Association, 76–78, 82
Dunlop, John, 153–155, 170–173, 177–179

Eisenhower, Dwight D., 138–139
Employee Representation Plans, 2–4
Esso, 41–42, 59, 85, 88
Esso Seamen's Association, 108, 109
Esso Shipping Company, 138
Esso Florence, 115–116, 119–120
Esso Houston, 127, 130
Esso Miami, 112
Esso New Orleans, 127, 130
Esso Philadelphia, 129–130
Esso Seattle, 72–74
Exxon, 13, 28, 30, 41, 64, 79, 114, 125–127, 132, 144

Flags of Convenience, 136, 138
Flags of Necessity, 136, 138

Gamble, M. G., 138
Getty, 13, 30, 42, 59, 79, 107, 109, 121
Getty Tanker Men's Association, 107–109
Getty Tanker Officers Association, 108

INDEX

Gompers, Samuel, 150
Green, William, 2

Hansen, Fred N., 32, 36–38
Hayek, F. A., 184, 187
Hettinger, Dwaine, 91, 131
Hoffa, James, 177
Humble, 64, 66–69, 71–72, 87, 90, 114, 118

Ingram Ocean Systems, 84, 86
Ingram Seagoing Officers Association, 84
Ingram Seamen's Association, 85
International Ladies Garment Workers Union, 162

Jacobs, Paul, 169
Jahre, Jorgen, 136
Jersey Standard Tanker Officers Association, 10, 41, 64–74, 82, 85, 87–89, 98, 112, 114–120, 125, 128, 130
Johnson, T. A., 117–120

Kennedy, Edward M., 142
Kennedy, John F., 137–139, 169
Kennedy, Joseph P., 13, 32
Kennedy, Robert F., 177–178
Kristol, Irving, 160–161

Labor and the American Community, 153–154
Landrum-Griffin Act, 154–155, 168, 177–179, 187
Learner, Laurence, 175–176
Lee, Victor, 157–158
Lewis, John L., 2–3, 18, 175–176

Marine Engineers Beneficial Association (AFL–CIO), 77–78
Maritime Administration, 143–144
Maritime Commission, 13
Masters, Mates and Pilots (AFL–CIO), 29, 89, 106
McClellan Hearings, 154, 177
McGrory, Mary, 175
McShane, John, 92
Meany, George, 1, 170, 172, 177–178
Merchant Marine and Fisheries, Congressional Committee on, 133, 145, 147
Merchant Mariner's (Seaman's) Document, 55, 92, 127
Miller, Arnold, 175–176
Mobil, 13, 30–31, 33–36, 40–57, 62, 79, 85, 100–104, 107, 141–142
Mobil Tanker Officers Association, 40–57, 100–104, 106–107, 121
Morrisey, James, 155
Motley, Constance Baker, 155
Murphy, John, 91, 131
Muskie, Edmund, 142

National Academy of Sciences, 136
National Industrial Conference Board, 3
National Labor Relations Board, 3–4, 18, 25, 107, 152, 167–168
National Maritime Union (AFL–CIO), 37, 59, 60, 79–80, 108–109, 155
National Research Council, 136
National Steel, 12
NATO, 136–137
Never Off Pay, 13
Newman, John Henry Cardinal, 158
New Republic, 171
Nixon, Richard M., 138, 140, 180
Norris-LaGuardia Act, 151, 179

OCAW, 101, 108
Opinion Research Corporation, 168, 173–174

Parker, Charles, 115–121
Pension bargaining, 40–76
Podhoretz, Norman, 160
Pollution, 114–121
Purcell, Theodore, S.J., 24

Raskin, A. H., 171
Reuther, Walter, 1, 162, 170, 172–173
Reynolds Metals Co., 84
Rockefeller Brothers Fund, 153
Roosevelt, Franklin D., 176
Rose, Antonio, 113

Saposs, David, 3–4
Seniority, 124–132

Shils, Edward B., 138
SIU, 109
Solzhenitsyn, Aleksandr I., 164
Special Sea Service Retirement Annuity Supplement, 68–69, 71
Staar, Louis, 127–131
Steel Workers Union (AFL–CIO), 12, 18–19, 20, 22
Stoddard, Frank, 91
Stulberg, Louis, 162–163
Sullivan, Leonor K., 145–147

Taft-Hartley Act, 7, 151, 174–175, 179
Taylor, Myron, 18
Teamsters Union, 152, 177–178
Texaco, 13, 17, 30, 42, 58–63, 85, 90, 95–99, 106–107, 115, 127
Texaco Radio Officers Association, 60

Texaco Tanker Officers Association, 18–21, 33–34, 58–63, 95–99, 100, 106, 115, 127
Townshend, C. S., 56
Trotta, Maurice S., 113
Troy, Leo, 23, 26–27

United Auto Workers, 4–5, 162, 170, 174–175
United Mine Workers, 2–3, 175–176, 178
U. S. Steel Corporation, 18

Wagner Act, 3–4, 179
Warner, Rawleigh, Jr., 141–142
Wire, Sydney, 120
Woodcock, Leonard, 162

Yablonski, Joseph A. (Jock), 175–176